THE CLERK

THE CLERK

My Thirty Six Years as Clerk of The Circuit Court and Comptroller of Holmes County, Florida

CODY TAYLOR

The Clerk, My Thirty-Six Years as Clerk of the Circuit Court and Comptroller of Holmes County, Florida

Self-published with CreateSpace by Cody Taylor
Books> Biographical Nonfiction

ISBN: 149929011X
ISBN 13: 9781499290110

Library of Congress Control Number: 2014908353
CreateSpace Independent Publishing Platform
North Charleston, South Carolina

Disclaimer: Many of the events described in this book are taken from the public records of Holmes County, Florida. If the author in his recollections deviates from the public records, he defers to the public record. The stories told and opinions expressed are for the enjoyment of the author's audience and as a personal legacy of family history.

Dedication

This book is dedicated to my grandparents, who gave me a chance at life, to my wife for sharing my life, and to my children and grandchildren for enriching my life.

ACKNOWLEDGEMENTS

I have so many to thank for help and encouragement in writing this book. The help of my wife Brenda to edit a somewhat unorganized manuscript and provide on-the-spot feedback was invaluable. Support from my children and grandchildren has been so rewarding. To all the deputy clerks who worked for me and were so loyal, I say thank you. Lastly, I want to thank the citizens of Holmes County for giving me the opportunity to be their clerk for thirty-six years. To God be the glory.

EPIGRAPH

Home is that familiar place you go for comfort and acceptance, through a collaboration of the mind and heart…literally…or in spirit.

"Holmes, my sweet home."

Table of Contents

FOREWORD

Holmes County is the place of my birth, and the place where I attended school, married, and chose to raise my family. It is the place that I cannot venture very far from. A trip of any length quickly turns into a yearning to go home, quite like a homing pigeon. Ultimately, when the Heavenly Father calls me home, my final resting place will be Holmes County, Florida.

Holmes County is situated in the central panhandle of Florida in what many refer to as LA, meaning lower Alabama. Its citizens are generally God-fearing and social conservative to the core.

The county has changed from its agriculturally dominated economy and is trying to catch up with the rest of the rapidly growing state of Florida. The influx of citizens from other parts of Florida and other parts of the United States has started to change Holmes County's political structure. Many of the county's brightest and best have left the area to find well-paying jobs. The state prison system operates a prison that has helped boost the job market in Holmes County and in several other surrounding counties. Interstate 10, which dissects the county, is beginning to have a favorable impact on the local economy.

Holmes County is in the more rural part of Florida, and its history is rich and colorful. The people are proud and independent, and many of the men and women have served in the armed services when called upon by their country. Those who joined the military or left for better employment opportunities seem to have a yearning to return to the county of their birth, to the natural, unviolated surroundings of the beautiful Choctawhatchee River and the rolling farmland and pine trees. Many of those native sons and daughters have returned to Holmes County to spend their retirement years.

It is my intent to share pieces of history and events from my thirty-six years as an elected official in a small rural county in northwest Florida. I hope to capture some of the charm and inviting nature of the county through my recollections and observations of people and politics. Hopefully others will gain a glimpse of the people and the place that have influenced and impacted my life, both personally and politically.

INTRODUCTION

I decided to write my memories as clerk of the circuit court of Holmes County, Florida, to leave a record for the citizens of Holmes County as well as for my family. Hopefully others will find the writings informative and amusing. The citizens of Holmes County gave me a front-row seat to watch and record the history of our county as it unfolded for thirty-six years. For this opportunity I will be forever grateful.

According to Judge E. W. Carswell's book, *Homesteading, A History of Holmes County*, I have the honor of being the longest-serving elected official in the history of Holmes County. Holmes County was created in 1848 when the Florida legislature was trying to reestablish the power balance between eastern and western counties. To give the western counties representation to offset the eastern counties being created, Holmes County was formed from portions of Walton, Washington, and Jackson counties. The new county had barely over one thousand people and had no public building other than churches. [i]

Being clerk of the courts, county recorder, and county auditor was never boring, since it involved so many areas of responsibility. It is within this context that I try to condense on paper some of the memories of my years in the clerk's office. In many cases I will cite from memory events that occurred that may or may not be substantiated by public records. If my recollection differs in any way from the public records, then certainly, I defer to the public record.

CHAPTER 1

First Taste of Politics

Early Interests

It was in the second grade in 1956 that I got my first taste of politics. My second-grade teacher told us that Dwight D. Eisenhower had defeated Adlai Stevenson for the presidency of the United States. That was where my interest in politics began.

Years later, as a teenage boy in the summer of 1964 on a Wednesday night, I slipped out of Pleasant Grove Missionary Baptist Church to listen to Barry Goldwater give the acceptance speech for the Republican nomination for president. The speech was at a place called the Cow Palace in San Francisco, and I listened to him on a car radio. I was only fifteen at the time and could not vote, but if I could have, it would have been for him. It was probably Goldwater more than anyone else who got me excited about public life.

High School Elections

As a junior in high school I first tested the political waters. I was elected president of the student council and the president of the local chapter of Future Farmers of America. My advisor was W. C. Revell, a gentleman for whom I had great respect. He had a profound effect on my future. He told me one day that he wanted me to enter the public speaking contest at the Holmes County Fair. He made me write the speech and practice it until I could say it without notes, then he took me to the contest in Bonifay at the county fair. There were speakers from the entire county, but when it was over, I had won my first public speaking contest.

Mr. Revell, who had been with Patton's army, kept us spellbound with war stories and life experiences. He had a saying that has stayed with me through the years. When someone offered an excuse, he would say, "Excuses only please the fellow who makes them." In my senior year he told me he wanted me to run for state office in the FFA. I did as he suggested and was elected first vice president of the Florida Association of the Future Farmers of America in Daytona Beach in the summer of 1967. Thankfully, I was able to schedule my year in a way that allowed me to play basketball in college and be a state officer. The experience of serving as a state officer provided me a head start when I later entered the political arena.

Since Mr. Revell was one of my favorite teachers I stayed in touch with him through the years. When he died a few years ago, his family asked that I do a eulogy at his funeral. I told them I would be glad to on behalf of all his former students. I broke out my old FFA jacket, and to my surprise I could still wear it after all those years. I told the crowd and his family the first rule he taught me about public speaking. He always said, "Stand up, speak up, shut up, and sit down." That is exactly what I did in tribute to his years of dedicated teaching. Somehow, I could feel Mr. Revell's approval.

* * *

CHAPTER 2

Running for Office

It was after the birth of our second son that several people approached me about running for property appraiser or clerk of the court. I first considered property appraiser. I contacted some people in the county about running for office. One of the people I contacted was a local attorney who was active in politics. I asked his advice on running for either property appraiser or clerk. He told me quickly that I might win the property appraiser's office but would be hard pressed to stay. He said folks get mad with the property appraiser and what I needed to do was run for clerk and I could stay there until I retired. The next day I contacted some politically active people on the west side of the county about running for clerk. I received encouragement everywhere I went.

I went home and told Brenda, and the two of us decided that I needed to run for clerk, and the rest is history. I also mentioned running for political office to another friend of mine, John Bomann. John was a cowboy who had come to Bonifay for the Kiwanis Rodeo, met a local lady, and married her and moved to Bonifay. I had coached one of his boys in little league, and his mother-in-law was one of my 4-H volunteers. When I told John that I was going to run for clerk he quickly said, "Cody, you are not a politician." I did not consider his comment a criticism. I agreed with him; I consider myself a good public servant and a poor politician.

In running for office I found out that candidates have to deal with several problems. The first problem involves things that people say about you that are not true. Usually these stories are started by the opposition. They may include such things as who is behind your running for the office or the unveiling of some dastardly deed you supposedly committed in your past. I found out the hard way that you cannot chase rumors during a campaign. Just go full speed ahead because tomorrow there will be a rumor about someone else that is bigger than the one about you.

The second thing that politicians have to deal with is bad things that people say about you that may be true. They might, for example, find out from your voting record that you have not voted on a regular basis, or that you do not own property. It is hard to talk about saving taxpayer dollars when you do not pay property taxes. Buddy Chestnut, a local feed-store owner and son-in-law of the late Judge Louis Hutchinson, tells a story about a guy running for county commissioner in Washington County. He came home one day and told his wife that his opponent was saying that he was guilty of stealing hogs. She looked at him and said, "Why does that worry you?" His response was, "Dang if they ain't going to prove it!"

The third thing a politician might have to deal with is having the press or the public not passing on information you wish they would. You would like someone to acknowledge the good job you are doing, or tell others how qualified you are for the job, or how much money you saved the taxpayers. Unfortunately, you don't always get the outcome or response you want.

Another important lesson you will learn quickly is that not everyone in politics will like you. The late Harvey Etheridge, a local life insurance agent and stepfather of county judge Owen Powell, once told me a story that I thought summed this up very well. He had a local radio program in the morning before he went out on his insurance route. He gave the local hospital report, the obituaries, and other news of the community. He had a big following and kept the public informed as to what was going on in the county. Harvey would announce on the radio each morning where he would be for lunch that day. He said he thought everyone loved him until he arrived at the home of a lady he was going to have lunch with. The family did not have air conditioning and had the windows up. As he got out of the car he overheard the lady say to her son, "There comes that fat Harvey Etheridge to eat with us." He said that made him realize two things: first that he needed to lose some weight, and second that not everybody liked him. So in politics, the sooner you realize that not everyone likes you, for whatever reason, the better off you will be.

I have one other interesting story about running for office. In 1976 Jimmy Helms, a local barber cut my hair on a regular basis. He shared the barbershop with his father-in-law, Mr. Joe Adams. The same week I announced my intentions to run for office, I went in to get a haircut from Jimmy, and the only barber left was Mr. Adams. As I walked in he said, "Cody, Jimmy is gone to lunch; sit down and let me cut your hair." Not wanting to hurt anyone's feelings during an election, I sat down in his chair. Mr. Adams was in his eighties and did not have a steady hand. He would have made a great army barber, because when he got through with you, you looked like you were headed for basic training. About the time he finished, Jimmy walked in, and I asked him if he thought I could win the election with this haircut. Jimmy said he was not sure if I could win the election with the haircut, but one thing was certain: I would not need another haircut until after the election.

Door to Door

In 1976 most Holmes County voters expected candidates to solicit their votes door to door. Using a county map, I would mark the road that I worked each day. I would work one side of the county for a couple of days and then go to the opposite side of the county. I kept moving around, marking my map and making notes as I went. I would start about nine every morning to make sure the voters were up, and I would go until bedtime. Brenda would prepare a lunch for me, and I would get in our 1971 Toyota without AC, stopping only for lunch and then continuing till nightfall. By the time the election came, I had marked out almost every road in the county and had gained some valuable insight into the county that I wanted to work for.

The Secret to Political Success

People often ask me what the secret of my political success is, and I will try to answer as simply and honestly as I know how. First and very important, hope you have a weak opponent. When I ran for clerk many people were generally mad with the clerk about his dealings with the county commissioners. People have told me that more people voted against the incumbent clerk than voted for me. That may or may not be correct. In 1988 the opponent who ran against me was so negative from the beginning that very few people paid any attention to him. He later was elected as a county commissioner, and he and I worked together civilly. In 1996 I had an opponent and looking back he was never much of a threat. He seemed to be more influenced by a few disgruntled citizens than by his qualifications to be clerk.

I had a friend who said there were two sure signs of a person getting ready to run for office. The first thing the prospective candidate would do is start paying bills. The second thing they would do is start going to church. Since I have gone to church most of my life I did not fall into that category, and thank the Lord I have always managed to keep my bills paid.

One important secret I discovered quickly was not to overlook the female voter. The first day I was knocking on doors I approached the door of an older couple and the man came to the door. I gave him my speech and turned to leave when a voice in the house said "Do you want my vote?" I stepped back on the porch as the lady came to the door and kindly explained that her husband did not tell her how to vote. She said if I wanted her vote I had to ask for it and if she thought I was best qualified, she would vote for me. I was embarrassed and it showed, but the lady did me a favor. From that point forward I always made sure I asked everyone, male and female, for their vote taking, none for granted.

Another secret to political success is to not let your opponent outwork you. I have had former officeholders tell me that they sat in the courthouse and got beat because some folks were telling them not to worry. Any time you have an opponent, you worry and you work. I went door to door each time I had an opponent. The hotter it was the better I liked it. I was always in better shape than my opponents and could take the heat. Folks love to see someone out working for reelection. I had friends who I knew would support me, but they were not disappointed that I had an opponent.

Another important thing for a politician to do is keep his ear to the ground. A few of my friends always made sure I did that. Ken Yates, who was my high school principal, always kept me up to date on what was going on around the county from his standpoint. He always gave me good political advice and has been the kind of friend that a person in public office needs to advise him. I never won an argument with him, but discussions with him helped prepare me to meet the everyday challenges of the clerk's office. Bill and Wyatt Parish, who owned a local hardware store, were good sounding boards also. People coming into their business all day, many times talking politics, gave them special insight as to how people felt about courthouse business and how it was being conducted.

Energizing the young vote is another important part of a successful campaign. Renn Vara, a young friend of mine, organized the young people for my campaign. Renn would gather a group to attend all the political rallies to lead my cheering section. He was an excellent political advocate. After I won he worked for me as a deputy clerk while he attended Chipola Junior College. He later got a job as an aide to Congressman Earl Hutto and finally ended up in California starting a very successful consulting business. He comes by to see us every now and then. During his most recent trip he was taking his daughter Alex to Boston to attend college in the summer of 2007. Alex participated in an internship for a semester in Holmes County in the fall of 2010. She went to court with my deputy clerks and did other jobs in the community to get a feel for what small-southern-town life was like where her dad grew up. I think her stay in Bonifay made her a little more conservative and helped her observe life from a different angle than she might have gotten in the San Francisco area.

During political campaigns, friends are valuable for many reasons. Friends can help put down rumors. Since way back at the beginning of my career someone has consistently started the rumor every few years that I was going to run for state representative. When Bob Crawford resigned as agriculture commissioner, Governor Chiles was considering whom to replace him with. The local paper ran an article saying that our state representative at the time, Sam Mitchell, was being considered as Crawford's replacement and I was on the list to replace Mitchell. No one from the paper or the governor's office talked to me about the matter. I guess it was a positive that people thought I was legislative material. What they did not realize was that the representative made about a fourth of what I made and I had children in college. That would never have been considered a good move from a financial standpoint. I would call around and tell a few of my friends that the rumor was not true, and they would start passing the word that I was staying on as clerk. Former county commissioner and good friend Ray Lewis always encouraged me to run for the legislature, but for the reasons previously stated I did not.

As clerk taking suggestions from others could be very helpful. When I first took office the county employees got paid on the first and the fifteenth of the month. County employees would literally come to the clerk's office and stand around to get their paychecks on payday. The first and the fifteenth would sometimes fall on the weekend or on holidays, and we had a time figuring out when to do the payroll. One of the foremen on the road crew, came to see me one day and asked me if I would consider going to an every-other-Friday payday, because that would eliminate many of the problems we were having. I thought about it for a minute, and then told him he had a good idea and that I would ask the board to approve the change. The change has worked well through the years and is still used today.

Looking back after retirement, I see political life from a different standpoint. I realize that in politics there is a rule that exists that I call the "rule of political reality." This rule basically says that when political opponents start telling untruths about you must have a plan to counteract the untruths. It can be seen playing out for any officeholder from City Hall to the county courthouse to Tallahassee and Washington. The basis of this rule came from a comment former commissioner Felton Miller made to me one day. Some folks in the county were not happy with some things the board had done and were complaining. Some of the complaints were ill founded. As usual they had thrown the clerk in with the board. Felton said, "Cody, we got to start some backfires." What he meant was to put the truth out to some supporters and let that meet the resistance by consuming the lies that were being told. Any politician who stays in office for any length of time will have to use this rule, "Start some backfires." In the last election cycle the Obama campaign took this rule to a new level. They used the social media to accomplish these tasks. It was very effective and seemed to catch the Romney campaign flatfooted. Candidates can use family and supporters to help set the backfires.

The one woman who has been the most influential in helping me in politics is my wife Brenda. The Lord blessed me with the perfect politician's wife. She is the opposite of me in dealing with politics. I am the worrier, and she is the one with the faith that all will be well. She always had an unwavering belief that God would take care of us even if I lost an election. When all the rumors of a campaign started, they never bothered her. When I had opposition and had to hit the road campaigning, she always took things in stride. She even found humor in some of my tactics. One day a lady on jury duty asked me how long I had been clerk, and I quickly answered her by saying, "It's like being married, I can't remember when I wasn't." She just laughed and told me how lucky I was to have her. Being the wife of a county official in a small county is no easy task. She served as my sounding board for all the problems that I would drag home and was always a source of encouragement when I needed it.

In addition to having the educational background and temperament, I think I had another intangible that many are not fortunate enough to have. Playing successfully on two state championship teams and being elected as a state FFA officer gave me good name recognition. All the rival county high school teams that I played against had huge followings, and even though they hated to defeated, they had a certain amount of respect for someone who could beat them fair and square. The first year that we won the state tournament we lost five regular-season games, and Bethlehem, one of the county schools, beat us three times. They were in a different class and were beat in the game before the state tournament. I had nothing but respect for those players.

Ponce de Leon was just as competitive and formidable. The second year we won the state tournament we lost two regular-season games, and one loss was to Ponce de Leon. They beat us the night before my grandmother and grandfather had their automobile accident. Playing basketball at a respectable level, being elected to a state FFA office, and later serving as the county 4-H coordinator gave me an advantage in my run for clerk.

TERMS

When I look back on my years in political life I realize that I have lived my life basically in four-year increments. When you are first elected, the time from election or reelection until the term begins is what I call the honeymoon period. You are completing a term and preparing for the next. You can relax and enjoy the last few months of a term. Then January comes and you begin the new term thinking it will be a long time before the next election. The years with no elections remind you that two years is a short span of time. Then you get into the third year, and before you know it it's qualifying time again. That's about the time the rumors begin—rumors of who wants to run against you

ELECTIONS

After taking office I did not have opponent until 1988. That year, a local businessman who graduated from Poplar Springs several years ahead of me decided to run. He obtained a copy of the county audit, which showed the county had had to repay the state $75,000 in FEMA funds from a hurricane that happened in 1975, before I took office. It was after I took office, however, that the board was forced to enter a payment plan to repay the funds. He took the audit and ran around the county telling people that I was responsible for the payback. Thank goodness his negative campaign got nowhere. In Ponce de Leon he got up to speak and said that he had crashed his crop-dusting plane in a field in the county and had survived. He then said he thought the Lord had left him here to be clerk. I was standing off to the side, and the thought went through my mind to change my speech. I wanted to say, "I did not know I was running against you and the Lord, because if I had, I would have certainly dropped out." My better judgment prevailed, however, and I gave my standard speech. When the votes were counted, I beat him in every precinct in the county.

I held office from 1988 until 1996 without another opponent. In 1996 I had a young fellow run against me. He ran a different campaign from my last opponent and never really got personal. I really felt sorry for him before the race was over. I beat him in every precinct in the county except his small home precinct. This campaign was probably the highlight of my political life. I handled the campaign pretty well, and my family and friends held me up. My boys kept trying to get me to say some things in my speech that I kept putting off. The local Democratic committee had rallies at several locations in the county, and the last rally was in Bonifay on the Saturday night before the election. The boys wanted me to end with a bang and had devised a speech that I finally agreed to use. My opponent's resounding theme was that it was time for a change and twenty years in office was enough.

I started out by thanking the people for letting me be their clerk for the past twenty years. I continued by saying my opponent thought anyone who had been in a job for twenty years or more should be fired. This would include bus drivers, teachers, doctors, and anyone else, because he says twenty years is enough. Then I went into the part the boys had written for me. I asked the crowd to imagine we were all on an airplane headed to New York and the pilot made his introductions and told the passengers onboard that he had been making this flight for twenty years and had never had a problem. I then described someone in the rear standing up and saying, "Wait a minute, there is a nice young fellow here who would like to fly this plane. He has never flown a plane before, but he is a nice fellow, and if you all will help me, we are going to throw the pilot off the plane and let this young fellow fly us to New York." I then asked, "How many of you are going to stay on the plane?" When I finished the last line, the message was loud and clear. I concluded, and the crowd went wild. My opponent spoke last that night, and he could hardly say his name. The boys had come up with a good idea, and it was well received to say the least.

I did not have an opponent in 2000, 2004, or 2008. The longest hour has to be the hour before qualifying ends. Months of rumors of who your possible opponents might be, evaporates and you have relief. Qualifying came and went on that day, June 20, 2008, and I was unopposed. It was a great feeling after all those years realizing that I would not go through another qualifying period before retirement.

TAKING OFFICE

In Florida the Joint Select Committee on Judicial Personnel of the Florida legislature has calculated that the clerk's office performs 926 different constitutional and statutory duties. I will discuss some of the different functions in detail.

The Clerk of the Circuit Court in Florida counties has a unique job in that it really involves several jobs grouped together. The clerk is the county recorder, county auditor, clerk of the county court, and clerk of the circuit court. Having fulfilled these jobs for the past thirty-six years, I have a unique perspective of the workings of county government. Obviously one person could not do all the jobs I mentioned. The clerk appoints deputy clerks to work in each of these areas. When people ask me how I do all the jobs, I always explain that I could not do it without good employees. I have found that the success of any public official will be measured by the competence and integrity of the people they employ.

Some personnel management classes teach that power in an organization comes either by controlling the checkbook or by overseeing the computer system. In a small county, the clerk of the circuit court controls both. The clerk also handles all the money, pays all the bills, and does payroll for all county employees. The clerk additionally has the responsibility of pre-auditing all county bills before paying them. The law states if a clerk approves a bill for payment that is not a legal claim against the county, the clerk is personally responsible for the bill. That was a huge responsibility that I never took lightly, and I personally approved each bill or had one of my department heads approve them if I was unavailable.

In January of 1977, I took office as the clerk of the circuit court for the first time. What a rude awakening! I was twenty-seven at the time and had to adjust quickly to the daily decisions of the clerk's office. I found out in a hurry that your employees can make or break you in a public office. Fortunately for me, I had retained Elizabeth Arnold and Sue Andrews from the previous clerk. I had also hired Melba Jackson, a lady I knew from Poplar Springs High School. Melba was my head bookkeeper for over twenty years until her retirement in 2003. Her honesty and sense of right and wrong were a good compass for keeping the clerk's finances above reproach. When she retired, Alice Vickers became the supervisor in the bookkeeping department and Kathy Lee took over as the bookkeeper for the clerk. They both had an impeccable sense of right and wrong that made them dependable employees.

Elizabeth Arnold was my chief deputy and administrative right arm for thirty-six years. I often kidded her about working for me for so many years without voting for me. She voted for her boss in 1976, and I did not have an opponent until 1988. She spent twelve years working as my chief deputy without having voted for me. I think she made up for that in 1988 and 1996.

Both she and Melba saw the clerk's office go from a literally manually run office with nothing mechanical except electric typewriters and calculators, to a fully automated, efficient office. Melba was from the old school, and change came a little harder for her than Elizabeth. Elizabeth's vision of needed improvements was to a large degree responsible for the clerk's office working smoothly. She convinced Melba and others that the changes were for the best and needed to be implemented. Elizabeth retired at the same time I did after having worked for over forty-two years in the clerk's office. I will always be grateful for her outstanding ability to help me carry out my duties as clerk.

Hiring good personnel is a must to run a public office. I put a policy in place for filling vacancies to help insure this goal. I advertised for the position, required the applicants to take a general knowledge test, and then selected the best-qualified person for the job. The test did not always tell me who to hire, but many times made it very clear who not to hire. In later years I gave the department heads and my chief deputy more input into the hiring process.

People received my hiring policies very well. Many were surprised by the test, which contained general knowledge questions that citizens should have been aware of. It was surprising how many citizens did not know the name of the governor of Florida or the population of Holmes County.

I had an opening some time ago in the bookkeeping department, and we went through the process that I described previously. The job included taking the minutes for the county commissioners. The department head did not feel good about any of the applicants. I told her to cull them all and start again if that was what she wanted to do. I always sent a letter to all the applicants telling them who got the job, thanking them for applying, and letting them know that their application would be kept on file for any future vacancies. We sent the letters, and the lady who was the top-ranked person of the group did something that I had never seen done before. She asked the supervisor if I would talk to her and explain to her why she did not get the job. I told her that I would meet with her and the supervisor and explain the process. She came in, we had a nice chat, and then she told us that she had applied for several jobs. She wondered if the reason she was not getting the jobs was because she had just moved to Holmes County from Michigan and talked like a Yankee.

My supervisor had told me before the meeting that she was having second thoughts about the young lady and thought I might need to rethink the job offer. As we talked, the young lady made an impression on me, and I told her that since she was bold enough to appeal my decision, I thought I would give her a chance. To begin with, she and I had to get use to each other's dialect. She had an obvious Yankee accent, and mine is strictly Southern. I told her one day I was going to get her some lessons in Southern language, and she told me she was going to get me some lessons in English!

Dealing with county commissioner meetings was a chore for her to begin with. Commissioners are notorious for making motions while someone else is talking yet expecting the deputy clerk to get down exactly what was said. She did very well, until one day out of the blue, one of the commissioners said, "It's time to call in the dogs and put out the fire." She came to me the next day and asked me what that meant, and I told her that was a motion to adjourn. She did very well on the job; her persistence prevailed.

Another key ingredient besides good personnel to help run an efficient office is good computer software. The most dramatic change with small clerks' offices software in Florida began in February of 2000. Clerks were having a meeting in Destin, Florida. Rickey Lyons, the clerk in Lafayette County, and I were talking about problems we were having with our current software provider. The person who provided software to a number of small counties was a sole operator and often traveled from county to county by motorcycle. None of the counties had his source code, and we constantly worried what we would do that if he wrapped himself around a telephone pole. We told Marsha Ewing, the president of the clerk's association, that we needed to have our own software solutions. She responded that she needed a civil package and would support the idea.

The three of us talked to the clerk's association executive director, Roger Alderman. He said there might be some federal funds available for the project. Florida Court Clerks and Comptrollers staff included Russ Curtis, Melvin Cox, Jim Cleek, and several programmers and support staff. They worked on the request for proposals from prospective vendors. The request for proposals called for the clerk's association to own the software totally, including the source code. We had several vendors interested, but only one, Systems Software Design, actually offered to sell their source code. Wayne McClellan, the owner of the company, had software running in several counties, and that made his offer very interesting. He offered to sell the software for $500,000, including the source code. He would help with all conversions and consult with the association to get everything operating.

There were fifteen or so counties that we felt this software would be ideal for, but the problem was that these were the smallest counties with the least amount of money to invest in software.

We came up with the idea of letting the Clerk's Service Corporation, which was a not-for-profit corporation used by clerks for various projects, loan the newly formed software group the money for the project. The transaction was handled by conference call. I was the spokesman for the software group. We had a great deal of support, but the chairman at the time did not seem to be sold on the new system. I gave the services group board of directors the background for the project and requested the loan. There was a lengthy discussion, and then Kendall Wade, the clerk from Franklin County, made a motion to approve the loan, and Jeff Burton, the clerk from Indian River County, a large county that did not need the software, offered a second. As the vote progressed it was evident it would pass. The chairman voted yes also, and it was unanimous.

We started with that SSDI software and a very capable, willing staff. Today the software owned by the clerk's association is called Clericus and is used in some form by over half the clerks of Florida. One of the most interesting proofs of the software's viability is that Manatee County has signed on and provided a great amount of funding for the package. Chip Shores, Manatee County Clerk, is one of the clerks who could purchase any software package he wanted for his office, as could several other clerks who are now on Clericus. It has been rewarding to see a dream come to fruition that you and a few of your fellow clerks initiated. The Clericus package is now recognized as first-class software and includes imaging for all facets of the clerk's office. It has an in-court processing module that has greatly reduced the court processing time for deputy clerks. The package is constantly being improved, and other clerks' offices are implementing the software on a regular basis.

I found out quickly that the Florida Court Clerks and Comptrollers was an organization that could be the salvation of small-county clerks. When I was first elected, I was a little dubious of the clerk's association, but through the years I have learned to lean on them for so many things. Ken Kent and the staff have gone out of their way to provide service to the clerks of Florida. Melvin Cox and the computer software developers have been successful in keeping clerks on the leading edge of technology. When The Affordable Health Act was rolled out in 2013 with all its problems, I could not help but think of the great job FCCC staff had done on Clericus. If

Melvin Cox and his staff had been given several hundred million dollars and three years they would have the health care system up and running with change to spare.

* * *

CHAPTER 3

CLERK OF THE COUNTY COURT

The part of the clerk's job that relates to the court system is also very interesting. Being clerk to both county court and the circuit court gives one the opportunity to be involved in every case filed in the county, including traffic, divorces, and all criminal cases. The clerk's office has access to every warrant that is issued before the person who is to be arrested is taken into custody by law enforcement. I have made it a policy through the years not to know about every divorce, traffic ticket, or restraining order that was filed. I saw people in the grocery store or the bank and they would ask me about their traffic case just as if I personally filed each one. Since there are hundreds of traffic, criminal, and civil cases filed each year, it would be literally impossible for me to be fully knowledgeable of each one.

The county court in Florida hears civil cases of up to $15,000. The types of cases in county court are landlord-tenant, small claims, regular county court civil and replevin actions. Criminal traffic cases and misdemeanors are also handled in county court. Deputy clerks file cases, collect filing fees, and keep a docket for all the different types of cases. Either the clerk or a deputy attends all the court hearings and all the trials. The clerk is required to keep the minutes of the proceedings in trials and deals directly with the county judge to ensure a smoothly operating court system.

As clerk of the county court I have always been fortunate to have good county judges who are easy to work with. I have had four resident county judges, Judge Louis Hutchinson; Judge Warren Edwards, who was appointed when Judge Hutchinson died in office in 1981; Judge Robert E. Brown, who retired in 2004; and my last county judge, Judge Owen Powell.

County Judges

The first county judge I will discuss is Louis Hutchinson. As I mentioned, years ago juries were selected from the list of registered voters. Each January the clerk's office would take the entire voter list and pick a thousand names and put them in the jury box. When a jury was needed I would take the box to the judge and he would pick the number of jurors he thought were needed. Judge Hutchinson was always straightforward and would say what was on his mind. As he drew the names he would elaborate about what kind of juror the person would be. He would say to me, "Cody, that guy would not vote to convict anyone." Or he might say, "This one would be all right."

He taught me many lessons about life in politics. The most important one of all was that it is better to be respected by the citizens than liked by them. He told me not to loan people money because they will take your money and vote against you. The judge said if you want to make an enemy, loan someone money, and they will cross the street to avoid coming into contact with you. Well, I did not take his advice and loaned a man, seventy-five dollars. Judge Hutchinson was right; he did not pay me back.

There was a custodian in the courthouse, Mr. Jesse, who loved politics. He also, on occasion, drove the man I had loaned the money to around to different places in town, because he did not have a car. Jesse came by one day and told me that he had taken the man to the grocery store and had asked him about politics in the county. The man told Jesse that if I had an opponent, I was going to get beat. I asked Jesse to take a message back to the man for me. I told him to tell the man if I got beat, I was going to start collecting all the money people owed me, and I was going to start with him. The next day Jesse came by to report. "The man you loaned the money to says he thinks you might make it one more term." I did take the judge's advice after this incident; I would buy someone food and clothes if they were in need, but I did not loan them money.

In the years of clerking for Judge Hutchinson not one time did I see him dismiss a case for political reasons; as a matter of fact the opposite was always true. He followed the dictates of the law, regardless of what the situation was. One day he and I were in his office discussing something of great importance when the only black deputy sheriff in the county came into his office. He told the judge he needed to talk to him about a traffic ticket he had written. He said he wanted the judge to dismiss the case. The judge found the case and told the deputy to raise his right hand. He proceeded to administer the oath as if the deputy were a witness. The oath was "Do you solemnly swear that the ticket you wrote was a lie and not the truth?" The deputy snatched his hand down and said, "Judge, it was the truth, but the sheriff told me to come over and have it dismissed." The judge told the deputy, "Now, you go back and tell the sheriff that this case is not going to dismissed."

The sheriff mentioned was Ben Jones, who had previously been the county tax collector but had given up the safety of that less-controversial job to successfully run for sheriff. He was an Andy Taylor–type sheriff who did not arrest someone unless he just had to. He and Judge Hutchinson were philosophically so far apart on how to handle lawbreakers that they often clashed; the judge wanted to go harder on the person, and the sheriff wanted to ease up. These clashes would last throughout the work day, but when we all went fishing down at Cypress Springs in Washington County their relationship would completely change. The judge, Supervisor of Elections Marlin Register, Deputy Lonnie Hagans, property appraiser Jack Faircloth, Mayor Robert Hall, Hulon King, Tamphus Messer, and I would go down late in the afternoon, fish, cook the fish, eat, and have a great time. The judge and the sheriff would be the best of friends while we were fishing, but the next day at the courthouse they would be back at it again.

The judge also introduced me to suckerfishing on Econfina Creek down in Washington County. Suckers are considered trash fish by many because they have so many tiny bones, making them very difficult to eat. However, if you slice them the right way, they are a very delicious-tasting fish. The judge organized a fishing trip that included Shay McCormick, Rickey Callahan and several elected officials. Judge Hutchinson's son-in-law, Buddy Chestnut, usually went along with us on these trips as well. He was, and remains, an avid outdoorsman. Lawrence Cloud, a local businessman, would also go along and always brought his wit and humor. We took some cooking utensils and cornbread mix for hushpuppies and headed down to Econfina.

In the spring the suckers come up the creek to lay their eggs on the sandy bottom. The water is clear most of the time, so the fish are easy to see. The judge had told us to bring Polaroid sunglasses to cut down on the glare. We walked up to some springs that were located in the creek, and we could see fish everywhere. The judge took a long, stiff fishing pole with a treble-snatch hook and dropped it in the water. (The snatch hooks were legal on this type of fish. The judge would not allow any illegal activity to go on with him in the crowd.) In just a second he had hooked a huge hen sucker and landed her. We began to fish and hooked into some whoppers. We caught fish until we had trouble carrying them out. There was no limit on how many suckers you could catch. We enjoyed many trips fishing and cooking on the banks of the Econfina Creek. Most of the land along the creek is closed to the public now, and the fading memory of suckerfishing on Econfina is dear only to those of us who were fortunate enough to have been there.

Someone mentioned to me one day that the courthouse officials were fishing too much. I mentioned the complaint to the judge, and his response was as usual straight to the point. He said, "Cody, the good Lord made the earth 80 percent water, so he expected man to fish a great deal more than to work." That seemed to settle the issue.

Another interesting thing Judge Hutchinson taught me concerned funerals. Some politicians thought you had to go to every funeral in the county. In addition to being there at the visitation and funeral, they felt as though they had to shake every hand in the house. Not the judge, though—his rule was simple. You only go to the funeral of someone you know well or someone you are kin to. Your visit should be to pay your respects and offer your condolences. You should not stop and politick along the way or shake any hands unless someone offers on the way out the door. You do not stop and politick in the yard; you get in your vehicle and leave. That is the policy that I have followed through the years. A fellow clerk in another county went to so many funerals that some people put it in their will that they did not want him at their funeral.

A classic Judge Hutchinson story concerned a local man who had a drinking problem. The man was arrested by the highway patrol and was carried to the Holmes County Jail for DUI. After the trooper left, the sheriff gave the man his keys and told him to go straight home. Several weeks later we called a jury for county court and had the man's trial. The prosecutor was a young man named Joe Sheffield. The defendant represented himself. After the state presented their case, the judge told the defendant that it was his turn. The man said, "Judge, what do I say?" The judge said, "Tell the jury your side." The accused stood up and addressed the jury with something along the lines of, "Ladies and gentlemen of the jury, it's true the highway patrolman picked me up for DUI and delivered me to the county jail. But ladies and gentlemen, as soon as the trooper left, the sheriff gave me my keys and told me to go straight home, and I did. Would he have done that if I was drunk?" With that said, the defendant sat down. The jury went out, and after a short period of time they came back with a "not guilty" verdict.

Home visits are unheard of for most judges but not Judge Hutchinson. He told me that he was home one night and got a phone call from a fellow who lived a short distance from him. The fellow was a veteran who had a drinking problem and was known to be rough on his wife from time to time. He had been before the court many times before for his misconduct. The man wanted the judge to come down to his house to see him and the judge agreed. Upon arriving the judge said the man was sitting at the kitchen table with a ketchup bottle broken over his head with blood and ketchup everywhere. The man looked at the judge and said, "Judge I just wanted you to see it was not always me." The judge said he had to laugh at the man's attempt to reassign blame. Making quick practical decisions was no problem for the judge. One day I was in his office and a gentleman from out of town was paying a traffic ticket. I noticed a fifty-dollar bill lying on the floor after the man left. I told the judge what I had found as we both watched the man do a U-turn in front of the courthouse. The judge, without missing a beat, said, "Cody, that money belonged to that fellow. Just add the fifty dollars on for the U-turn he just did."

Judge Hutchinson was a man known for being direct and to the point. This is a story that exemplifies how straightforward he could really be. A fellow judge from Walton County, Joe Dan Trotman, called Judge Hutchinson to go to Tallahassee with him to lobby the legislature. The judges met with a legislative committee, and one of the judges got right to the point by requesting a pay raise for all the judges. The judges all chimed in, agreeing that they needed a raise, all except Judge Hutchinson. One of the legislators noticed that he had not said anything and asked him, "Judge Hutchinson, what do think about the raise?" Judge Hutchinson responded in his usual straightforward way by saying, "I knew what the salary for county judge was when I ran for office, and I am happy with the pay." He said Judge Trotman let him off at the courthouse that afternoon and made it clear that that would be the last time he would ask him to lobby the legislature for a raise.

In addition to getting to the point in short order, Judge Hutchinson was also brutally honest. There was a farmer who owed the judge money for feed he had purchased from the judge's feed store. The man had owed the money for several months and came in just before he qualified for school board to pay the judge his debt. He came by several times during the election to buy different things, paying in cash, thinking he would get the judge's support. The man got beat badly and got only three votes in the judge's precinct. The man came by and mentioned the three votes that he got. The judge looked at the fellow and told him he was sure his cousin and his wife had voted for him, but he just could not figure out who the other person was.

Asking Judge Hutchinson to be a character witness could be tricky if your character was less than stellar. A local man got arrested in Georgia, so the father of the young man asked Judge Hutchinson to be a character witness for his son. Judge Hutchinson, as only he could reply, said, "I'm afraid I can't do that; I really don't know anything good I could say about your boy." The guy decided he probably would not need the judge as a witness.

Judge Hutchinson was not an attorney but did have an attorney run against him once. The local attorney ran for judge when Judge Hutchinson and Judge Brown were both running in 1976. Judge Hutchinson won the election and served until his death. Later I moved into the same office in the courthouse that Judge Hutchinson once occupied. Occasionally, it seemed, as I searched for answers, that the judge gave me just the right answer to the problem I was dealing with. Sometimes one of my deputy clerks would refer a problem to me, and when the person left, the deputy clerk would ask me what happened. Many times I recall telling them, "I let Judge Hutchinson talk to them."

Judge Warren Edwards was a retired circuit judge from Orange County, Florida, who retired to Holmes County and opened a part-time law practice. When Judge Hutchinson died in office, the governor appointed Judge Edwards to serve until the next general election. Judge Edwards was the county's first lawyer judge and was easy to work with and was a very effective judge. He chose not to run in the next election, and Judge Brown was returned to office.

Judge Robert E. Brown was elected county judge after the death of Judge Hutchinson. For more than twenty years he was my county judge. He was a laid-back individual who always thought the public deserved more than an equal shot at justice from the judge. He always tried to help people. He operated under the theory that cooperation between the county judge's office and the clerk's office was vital to the efficient operation of the county court system. Judge Brown was the last non-lawyer judge to serve in Holmes County. The Florida legislature some years before decided that all county judges in Florida would be required to be lawyers. However, anyone who was serving as judge when the law passed could be grandfathered in. Judge Brown was in that category. He put on his political signs "Non-lawyer, the people's judge." He stayed in office until he retired.

Judge Brown always opened court with prayer and for many years required people he placed on probation to attend church regularly. Some folks complained to the chief judge, who met with Judge Brown and told him that he could not require probationers to attend church. He stopped making probationers go to church but never quit praying before each session of court.

I never saw Judge Brown get upset regardless of the situation. When he was serving on the canvassing board during the disputed 2000 election, the attorney for the losing sheriff candidate called him to the stand and harassed him excessively. She even asked him what medications he was on. He gave her a whole list, and then she asked if he thought that the meds he was on affected his ability to think. He just calmly answered her with a no and continued, unfazed by her antics. The attorney some weeks later got a traffic ticket in Holmes County and had to appear before Judge Brown. I wanted him to assess the maximum fine, but Judge Brown gave her the minimum and treated her like a family member. She, in the meantime, was filing documents with the district court of appeals alleging all the Holmes County elected officials were corrupt.

Judge Brown was also a good storyteller. Once he told the story about some of his relatives inviting the preacher home after church for Sunday dinner. They were drinking milk with the meal, and a relative fixed his drink with a little nip of moonshine. When he placed the drinks on the table he got his and the preacher's glasses mixed up. It was a large glass, and the story goes that the preacher drank the whole glass and could not quit bragging about how good the milk was. He finally asked the man if he would be interested in selling the cow. The relative told him that he couldn't sell the cow since it was the family's only source of milk. The pastor then made him promise that if he could not sell him the cow he would sell him the first female calf.

Judge Owen Powell replaced Judge Brown upon his retirement as county judge and become Holmes County's first elected attorney county judge. He had practiced law in the county for many years and was always easy to work with. He and I were personal friends as well as coworkers. Judge Powell made the clerk's office run much more efficiently since he could handle all types of cases, both county and circuit. He presided over restraining orders for many years and handled probate matters. His judicial assistant, Cheryl Hammond, was very helpful to the clerk's office in keeping cases moving through the system. Judge Powell's easy manner and laid-back approach was a good fit for serving as county judge and acting circuit judge.

Interesting County Court Cases

One interesting county court case involved a donkey. A local man loaned his donkey each year to a friend who ran a cane mill on Highway 90 east of Bonifay. One night the donkey got out of his makeshift pen and wandered onto Highway 90 and met a semi-truck head on. Needless to say a donkey is hardheaded, but he lost that encounter. The borrower told the owner what had happened to his donkey and promised to replace the animal. He found a donkey, bought it, and gave it to the owner. The owner was a trusting fellow and had no reason to think that he would ever need to prove the donkey was his. The donkey borrower died a while later, and his wife called up the owner and told him she wanted her donkey back. The owner explained that the donkey was his. She told him that she had the bill of sale and would sue him to get the animal if she had to. He told her to do whatever she had to do. She filed suit, and Judge Robert Brown, the county judge at that time, heard the case. After taking testimony, Judge Brown awarded the donkey to the borrower's widow. The donkey owner never got over losing his donkey in this circumstance.

We once had a dog case in county court that almost finished off the entire clerk's office. A gentleman from Holmes County saw an ad for a registered miniature boxer bulldog. The lady who owned the boxer pups lived in Madison County. The man called and set a time to go look at the dogs. He liked the dog and decided he would purchase one for the set price of five hundred dollars. He paid her the money, but she insisted on a signed agreement that spoke of some general rules regarding how the dog was to be treated. The man did not notice a clause in fine print that said something to the effect that the dog could not be kept in an outdoor pen but had to be raised in the home of the purchaser and made part of the family.

The man took the dog and put it in his outside dog pen with his other dogs. The lady who had sold the dog showed up at the man's home one day, unannounced, and took photos of the dog in the pen. She then went to the sheriff's department and asked them to go with her to retrieve the dog because the man had breached the agreement. The sheriff's department told the lady that this was a civil matter and she would have to go to the clerk's office to file the necessary paperwork. This was where our nightmare began. For the next several months she made our lives miserable. She first demanded that we tell her how to file her suit. My deputies finally got me involved because they could not deal with her. I explained that we could not be her attorney but that we would file anything she wanted us to. She finally told me she wanted to file a replevin and that she did not have the money to pay the filing fee. I let her file as an indigent, and the case progressed to a hearing before County Judge Owen Powell. He ruled against the woman, who actually wanted the dog returned to her and wanted to keep the money as well.

The lady was so upset with the verdict that she called everyone from the ACLU to the governor to complain about how she had been mistreated in Holmes County. She contacted an attorney, who told her to file for a rehearing and to file a motion to have Judge Powell recuse himself since she was convinced was that he was prejudiced against her. He granted her motion to recuse himself, and the chief judge appointed Judge Woody Hatcher to handle the rehearing.

The day for the rehearing finally arrived. After taking testimony, Judge Hatcher came to the same conclusion that Judge Powell had and told her that in open court. The lady threatened to appeal but never did. Be warned; if you see an advertisement for the purchase of miniature boxers from Madison County, Florida, beware!

Jury Selection

The clerk's job included selecting juries for trials. The judge would determine the number of jurors for each week of trials. He would then instruct the clerk's office to summons the jurors. The process included printing the jury notices and mailing them to the jurors.

A computer using a random selection program selects juries for all courts from the driver's license database. The interesting thing about these jury lists is that they are organized by zip code. Ponce de Leon, Florida, has the same zip code as Red Bay, Florida. Red Bay is in Walton County, so citizens there cannot serve on our juries since they are not Holmes County residents, but they are not on Walton County's jury list because they have a Holmes County zip code. To this day the Division of Drivers Licenses in Tallahassee has not solved the matter of getting these people in the correct county.

When I first became clerk, juries were selected from the voter lists. Many people would not register to vote to avoid serving on a jury. The law was later changed to selecting juries from the driver's license list. The Florida Legislature wanted a better cross section of jurors and the driver's license list provided that. All the judges for whom I have clerked have requested that the clerk's office handle the juror excuses. I have dealt with most of the excuses through the years, and some of them were very interesting, to say the least.

The law allowed me to excuse anyone over the age of seventy or anyone who had a doctor's excuse. Prospective jurors could also ask to be postponed until the next term of court for any reason. Jury duty in Holmes County began with the clerk swearing in the jury for general competence. There have been very few times that I did not personally address the jury pool myself. My chief deputy,

Elizabeth Arnold, would be on hand to keep a record of the excuses and revise the final list while I spoke to the jury.

On one occasion I had instructed the jurors of acceptable excuses. An elderly lady raised her hand and asked me how much we paid if she stayed. I told her the pay was fifteen dollars. With obvious disdain she replied, "That won't even buy me fish bait." I explained that the amount was set by the Florida legislature, so she agreed to stay.

Here are a few of the excuses that I have gotten over the years: I do not want to judge anyone. I am too old. I cannot hear well enough. I have my own business and will have to close it if I serve on jury duty. I am a supervisor, and if I am gone no one else gets to work. I work offshore and will be gone. I am a trucker and will be on the road. I do not believe the judicial system is fair, and I will not vote to convict anyone. Medical excuses were always well used, too: I am on some drug that affects my reasoning ability, and, I am taking medicine and cannot hold my water. That was always a good one.

* * *

CHAPTER 4

Clerk of the Circuit Court

Circuit court judges

The circuit court jurisdiction covers any civil action over $15,000, any felony, and most family law cases.

The judges whom I have dealt with through the years in the circuit court, for the most part, were honorable people. My first circuit judge was Judge W. L. Bailey from Calhoun County. He was the only circuit judge I ever worked with who had an open-door policy. He would see anyone about anything. If someone wanted to see him about a case he was handling he would tell them that he could not have ex parte communication with them without the other side being present. If he was contacted he would announce the fact to both sides at the next hearing.

Judge Bailey's main office was in Blountstown, and he came to Bonifay usually once a month. There was no full-time assistant state attorney or public defender. The local court consisted of the clerk, the deputy clerks, the bailiff, a part-time prosecutor, and the judge. Judge Bailey moved after several years to serve in Calhoun and Gulf Counties. He was shot and killed several years later by a distraught ex-husband in a divorce case in the Gulf County courthouse. Judge Bailey always showed a great deal of wisdom in his handling of cases. There was one young defendant whose criminal record began in grade school with the juvenile system. Law enforcement arrested the juvenile time after time, bringing him before Judge Bailey on several occasions. This continued from grade school until the young man reached adulthood. Judge Bailey gave him every chance in the world, and finally, when he was eighteen, he was arrested for some offense and was brought before Judge Bailey again. The charge violated his probation, and the judge prepared to sentence him to the Department of Corrections for the first time. He looked over at the defendant and said, "Son, I have raised you in the court system, and I have done a poor, poor job." With that said, he sentenced the young man to the state prison system.

Judge Bailey was also a man you could talk to. Our church participated in a jail ministry at the Holmes County Jail. As a young deacon in the church, I was asked to take part in this jail ministry. Several deacons and I went together to the jail and talked to the prisoners. We became acquainted with one of the prisoners, Jerry Yarbrough. He was in jail for possession of moonshine whiskey. He only had three gallons when he was caught. He pled guilty to the charge thinking he would get probation. He caught Judge Bailey on a bad day, however, and the judge gave him three years in state prison. Jerry had a wife and several children. At the time of his arrest, he was working with a construction firm in Chipley, Florida. Jerry told us about his family and how he did not know what his wife was going to do with him gone. We just listened and never promised to do anything.

The next day Judge Bailey was in Bonifay and I talked to him about Jerry Yarbrough. I told him I thought that he had been too hard on Jerry and mentioned his wife and children. The judge asked, "Cody is this one of your Sunday school boys?" I told him that he was. He thought a minute and told me that he would reconsider and let Jerry serve time on the weekends in the county jail, but I was to say nothing to him at that time. He wanted him to worry about his sentence until the day he was supposed to be transferred to prison. That day was the next Friday, and on Thursday, the judge sent for Jerry to be brought to the courthouse. He told Jerry that he had reconsidered because his Sunday school teachers thought he deserved another chance. He told him that he was going to give him that chance but to be sure that he did not appear before him again. The judge changed his sentence to eleven months and twenty-nine days in the county jail to be served on weekends. That Christmas I got a card from Jerry's wife and all the children thanking me for helping Jerry. The best thing about that was Jerry never got in trouble with the law again and lived the rest of his life as a law-abiding citizen.

There were several other circuit judges I worked with over the years. I will comment on each of them, not necessarily in order of their service. N. Russell Bower was our judge for one year. His rulings created a situation that resulted in an attorney from Tallahassee requesting that the board of county commissioners and me be held in contempt of court. A defendant named Clark was accused of murdering a young teenage girl in our county while working as an exterminator. The family hired an attorney and paid him all they could borrow on their home, which was alleged to be $25,000. Before trial the attorney petitioned the court to be appointed a special public defender and have the county pay some of his fees. The county objected, and the judge ordered the Holmes County Board of County Commissioners to pay around $22,000 to the defense attorney.

The commission chairman at the time was H. R. Harrison. He refused to have the county consider paying the bill. The defense attorney filed a motion to hold the board and me in contempt. Gerald Holley, the county attorney, and former justice James Adkins of the firm of Carson and Adkins were our attorneys. The word had gotten out in the county that the judge was thinking of putting the whole board and the clerk in jail for refusing to pay the attorney. The date of the hearing arrived. Judge Bower entered court that day and was surprised at the huge crowd. He addressed those in the courtroom before the hearing began, saying that he was only doing what Florida law instructed him do, so any anger should be directed at the Florida legislature. Judge Bower was really on the spot; if he decided to hold us all in contempt he most likely would have had a riot on his hands.

It seemed that all of sudden he got a revelation from above on how to proceed. He told the lawyer he was denying his motion to hold the six of us in contempt, but would, in the alternative, give him a judgment against the county. With that said Judge Bower slipped out the back door. The defense attorney had his judgment and again requested that the county pay it. The commission and I refused again. The lawyer took the judgment and got the judge to sign an order of garnishment against the county's general fund. The local banker called and told me he had received the order and must send the money to the attorney. The lawyer got his money and then asked the judge to let him off the case. The public defender took over and tried the case. Judge Bower stayed with us only one year, and after this fiasco, he was ready to leave "The Ridge." That was what Bay County judges called the Holmes, Washington, and Jackson Counties portion of the Fourteenth Judicial Circuit.

Judge DeeDee Costello was appointed as a circuit judge during the time Governor Graham was running for the US Senate. The county attorney for Holmes and Washington Counties, Gerald Holley, was also one of the finalists for the appointment. Travis

Pitts, who was then the clerk in Washington County, and I went to Tallahassee to see Governor Graham to put in a good word for Mr. Holley, whom we both held in high regard. The governor was not in, so we saw Lieutenant Governor Wayne Mixon. We told him we would appreciate the governor considering Mr. Holley as the appointee. He was courteous to us, but when the governor made the appointment, he appointed DeeDee Costello. She spent a year with us, and it was turbulent at times.

A lady came by the clerk's office one day and asked one of the deputy clerks where the circuit judge's office was. Like many times before, she told her. In just a moment Judge Costello stormed in demanding to see me. She wanted to set one thing straight: we were not to send citizens up to her office, and she would not see anyone without an attorney. When she finally said everything she wanted to say, I told her what happened. Apparently she knew of my friendship with Mr. Holley, and after what seemed a long year she went back to Bay County. Through the years she seems to have mellowed and is now what I consider one of the most respected circuit judges we have on the bench. The days when a circuit judge would see the public like Judge Bailey did, however, were gone forever.

Judge Clinton Foster was with us one year on The Ridge. Judge Foster was the finest circuit judge I ever worked with. My deputy clerks and I were his clerks if we goofed he covered for us. The deputy clerks loved him. Putting Judge Foster in charge of training new circuit judges statewide could have greatly reduced the number of judges needed. Time did not mean anything to him; he started early and stayed late. He pushed lawyers to finish cases and did not let them drag on.

Judge Foster handled the divorce case of a former mayor and his wife, and the two sides would not agree on the division of property. The judge ordered me to sell their home on the courthouse steps. At the sale, the wife and their two children stood on one side, and the man, alone, on the other. The man finally won the bid at $90,000. On a partition sale the person has ten days to put up the money, and since he owned half the property he only had to put up $45,000. On the tenth day the banker who was loaning the man the money called and told me that for loan purposes he could not put up the money until the morning of the eleventh day. I told him that was fine. The morning of the eleventh day the money was paid. Shortly thereafter the wife's attorney filed a motion to set the sale aside because the man had not put the money up within the ten days.

This case shows that the law and common sense do not always coincide. I had to attend the hearing to set the sale aside. Judge Foster agreed to set the sale aside if the wife would bid more than her husband had. The wife said she would. The judge added, "If the woman does not put up the new amount in three days I will confirm the man's bid." The woman did not put up the money, and we gave the man a certificate of title to the property. I saw the man in the courthouse shortly after, and he was still upset with the way things had gone in his divorce case. He told me that his wife had two lawyers: "I hired her one and she hired herself one." He then proceeded to tell me what a poor job his lawyer had done. It is not unusual for both parties to be dissatisfied in a divorce case.

We had two other circuit judges who served with honor. Judge Don Sirmons and Judge Michael Overstreet had what I call the authoritative look of a judge and ruled with dignity and honor. Judge Sirmons retired, and Judge Overstreet still serves today.

Judge Russell Cole, a local attorney, was appointed circuit judge and a year later became our first resident circuit judge. The clerk's office had worked with Judge Cole for years when he was a private attorney, so we had no problem working with him in his new role.

Judge Hentz McClellan was our judge for one year. He was a very dignified and honorable judge. One day I had to be in his office for a hearing. I was there because a lady had filed an objection to a foreclosure sale that had taken place a few weeks before. She was the plaintiff and had been present at the sale with another woman and had actually bid on her own property. The fellow handling the sale for the bank was a processor server from Gadsden County, Florida, and a former clerk there. I had not seen the man in years, so we spoke and shook hands before the sale.

During the sale process server interrupted and told the bidders that he was willing to go to a certain dollar amount if he had to, so the ladies quit bidding. After the sale the women began telling people that I was in collusion with the process server and that he had intimidated her to stop bidding at the sale. The crazy thing was, under Florida law, she could have redeemed the property at any time up until ten days after the sale took place. It would have been redeemable for the amount she owed the bank plus attorney fees and court costs. Apparently the bidders thought they could buy back the property for a lesser amount than was owed the bank. The defendant bidder filed an objection to the sale. The judge held a hearing, and I had to be present. The attorney for the bank called me as the first witness and asked me if I had followed Florida law in handling the sale, and I indicated that I had. He asked me if the lady ever offered to redeem the property, and I told him no. The judge gave the lady an opportunity to say something. She had nothing to say other than the process server and I had done her wrong. The judge then asked the lady if she was prepared to pay the full amount she owed today, and she told him she could not. The judge denied her objection, and she walked out. Even though I was proven to be right, it was never a good feeling when the property being sold was someone's home.

Judge Allen Register was not only my circuit judge; he is also my first cousin. His father was my mother's brother. He graduated from the University of Florida law school and was the first member of our family to become a lawyer. He worked with the state attorney's office until he ran for judge in Washington County. He ran unopposed and was reelected until he was appointed to the circuit bench by Governor Jeb Bush. We grew up as next-door neighbors and went to church together.

Prior to becoming a judge, Judge Register was a very successful prosecutor. The only case that I remember him losing in Holmes County was a case involving alligator hunting. Alligators were put on the endangered list by the Florida Game and Freshwater Fish Commission. Coincidentally, the late Judge E. W. Carswell, a local historian, wrote a fictional story about a huge alligator called Two-Toed Tom who made his home in Sand Hammock Pond, just south of Esto, Florida, a small town in north Holmes County. The story was written to promote a local festival that Judge Carswell and others in the community had started. Some boys in South Alabama, seeing the story and thinking it was real, decided to take a small boat, a six-pack, a gun, and a light and go to Sand Hammock to kill old Tom. A game warden happened to be in the vicinity and, seeing the lights at night, decided to investigate. He caught the boys and arrested them for attempting to take alligators. One of the boys pled guilty, but the other one wanted a trial. It was obvious that the boy was guilty, but the jury verdict came in not guilty. Many of the jurors had experienced problems with gators at some time in their lives and did not hold the same sentiments for gators as the Florida Game and Freshwater Fish Commission.

The last Circuit Judge that I worked with was Judge Chris Patterson, from Bay County. Never did I see a judge more prepared for court and the cases he handled than Judge Patterson. He operated his court with dignity and efficiency and the court system operated smoothly under his watch. He is still the presiding judge in the county today.

I have, on occasion, dealt with judges from other counties. Judge McCrary, a judge from Jackson County, usually kept things interesting when he filled in. He was on the bench one day conducting child support hearings. The first case involved a woman who had filed a contempt citation against her ex-husband for not paying child support. During the hearing the man was relating a hard-luck story about being out of work and having another family. The woman got the impression that the judge was not going to do anything to her ex-husband, and she smarted off to the judge about his inaction. The judge calmly looked over at the woman and said, "Lady, I'm doing the best I can with what you married." He then sentenced the man to the county jail until he started paying the support.

Judge Michael Miller was the senior judge who handled the disputed sheriff's case of 2000 after Judge Foster retired. Judge Miller was from South Florida and had just moved to the area following his retirement. He knew very few people in Holmes County and did not care what they thought of him or his decisions. He handled the case very efficiently and fairly. He kept the attorney for the former sheriff in check and did not let her intimidate witnesses the way she usually did. He saw through the theatrics and made his decision based on the facts of the case and Florida law.

Trouble in the Courtroom

After the real estate crash in 2007 the Florida legislature started making budget cuts, and the judiciary received some substantial budget cuts. Clerks were spared the big cuts that others were getting because of the system that was established by the legislature. The system was designed to allow the clerks to retain their independence but at the same time be accountable to the legislature and to the Florida chief financial officer. Some judges could not stand the fact that the clerks had a system that seemed to insulate them from the same cuts the court was experiencing. The judges got a representative from Broward County to file a bill with the legislature to take the court-related duties of the clerk of the court and move them to court administration.

The bill also found a senate sponsor, so the fight was on in March of 2009 to save the elected clerks. Elected clerks have been a part of Florida government since its inception. The original delegates to the Florida Constitutional Convention in 1838 made provisions for election of the clerk. This has been in the Constitution for over 170 years. A former chief justice of the Florida Supreme Court testified before the Senate Judiciary Committee in February of 2009 that the court needed to have an appointed clerk, just like the federal court system. Thankfully the Florida legislature saw the power grab for what it was and did not buy into the judge's scheme.

Circuit Court Cases

The clerk is responsible in all court cases to assist the judge to make the courtroom operate efficiently. It was my job to question the jurors as to general eligibility, swear witnesses, keep minutes of the proceedings and mark and secure all evidence that was entered. The clerk also handled all appeals if there was one. With these jobs as a background I will discuss some of the more publicized cases that I recall.

Otis Toole and Henry Lee Lucas were two serial killers who confessed to murdering numbers of women throughout the United States. They were charged with the murder of two women in Holmes County. The murders, a few miles apart and seemingly unrelated, shook the whole county to the core. No arrests were made for many months, and finally a new sheriff, Thomas Strickland, promised to reopen the murder cases. Toole was imprisoned in South Florida, serving a life sentence for the murder of another woman. Lucas was imprisoned in Texas awaiting the death penalty for the murder of a woman in that state. Toole and Lucas were both indicted by a Holmes County grand jury and brought back to the county for arraignment.

Both men were totally unconcerned as the charges were read to them. They were then taken to Jackson County, Florida, where a Jackson County grand jury had indicted them for the murder of Jackson County sheriff Johnny McDaniel's father. The public defender's office was handling the Toole case, so Lucas was appointed a private attorney, for whom the county was going to be required to pay. As the cases progressed, Toole said he committed the murders and would plea, but Lucas said they did not commit the murders and he wanted a trial. The county commissioners in both Jackson and Holmes Counties asked the state attorney not to try Lucas in the two counties. It would have been a huge expense to the counties. If he was found guilty he would have been sent back to Texas to be executed. The state attorney showed some political backbone and sent Lucas back to Texas. Lucas signed a waiver agreeing that if Texas did not execute him he would come back to Holmes County to be tried. Toole pled and was sentenced concurrently with his life sentence he was already serving. George Bush, as governor of Texas, commuted Lucas's death sentence to life. Texas law enforcement became convinced that Lucas did not commit the murders he had confessed to in Texas. Thank goodness he died before he could be brought back to Holmes County. Toole also died while serving his sentence in the Florida system. In December of 2008 I read the announcement that Toole was believed to be the killer of Adam Walsh.

A more recent and humorous story from the circuit court involved a man being represented by my son, Luke. The client had been arrested for growing marijuana. The family had contacted the state attorney and wanted the boy to plea if the state attorney would agree to probation. Luke, having worked as an assistant state attorney, advised the family that he could not let the man plea without getting the results from the drug analysis from the Florida Department of Law Enforcement. The family was a little irritated with Luke but agreed to listen to him. They did not know that a hurricane had badly damaged Pensacola and also completely destroyed the FDLE lab where the drugs had been sent. When Luke demanded that the state produce the results, they could not, and the case was dismissed. Luke was sitting in court with the man when the state announced a nolle prosequi. The man looked over at Luke and asked, "Hey, Luke, how many years do I get for that?" Luke explained that he was free to go, as the case had been dismissed. The man, obviously relieved and excited, thanked Luke and told him, "Now that's the way to handle a case!"

Another murder case of note was the case of Thewell Hamilton. Hamilton was a Vietnam veteran who was accused of killing his wife and stepson. The prosecutor of the case was Allen Register. The judge was Fred Turner from Panama City, who was a colorful character and liked to be the center of attention. On the trial's opening day, I told him that a class from one of the high schools would be present in the courtroom. He grabbed his robe and went out and lectured the students for a long time on everything from the court system to his days in China with the Flying Tigers before World War II.

The state had only circumstantial evidence against Hamilton. There were no fingerprints or DNA on the murder weapon. The only witness was a three-year-old who could provide no information regarding the crime. Hamilton testified that an intruder killed his wife and stepson but could not explain why the intruder did nothing to him. After hearing the testimony, the jury found Hamilton guilty of first-degree murder. During the penalty phase, testimony was taken and the jury recommended the death penalty. The judge does not have to take the recommendation of the jury on the second phase, and the verdict need not be unanimous. While the jury was making its report to the judge, the defense attorney noticed one of the jurors, a young man, had taken a racing magazine back to the jury room. He asked the judge for a mistrial on the second phase, and Judge Turner granted his motion.

The state appealed, and since this was a death penalty case it went to the Florida Supreme Court. The court overturned Judge Turner and said that the magazine did not prejudice the jury against Mr. Hamilton. It took over two years for the Supreme Court to render its decision. Judge Turner had retired, and Judge Clinton Foster was appointed by the chief judge of the circuit to handle Hamilton's sentencing. The case was further complicated by the fact that the Florida Supreme Court had lost several pieces of the evidence, including the murder weapon, a pump shotgun. The court was unable to blame the clerk's office in Bonifay for the lost evidence because we had the UPS receipt signed by a court employee.

Judge Foster took the jury's recommendation of the death penalty. Hamilton's attorney's appealed, and his death sentence was overturned. He was sentenced to life in prison. The fact that he was a Vietnam veteran seemed to weigh heavily on the Florida Supreme Court.

One of the saddest cases we had was the murder case of Deputy Lonnie Lindsey. Deputy Lindsey was off duty and heard on his department radio about a robbery in progress at a liquor store close to his home. He got in his vehicle and began searching for the persons who committed the robbery. He spotted two individuals working on a truck by the side of the road. He stopped to check them out, and they opened fire on the deputy. Lindsey returned fire but was eventually shot and killed by Roy Lee Hall and Terry Ray. The two outlaws took off, leaving Lindsey mortally wounded by the side of the road. A backup deputy arrived as the two killers were leaving and alerted other deputies, who set up a road block for Hall and Ray. Hall had been shot in the hand by Deputy Lindsey, and as the two approached the roadblock they skidded to a stop and surrendered without a fight.

The trial for both of these individuals was moved to Bay County because of the publicity in Holmes County. Ray was tried first, and he was convicted and sentenced to death. Hall was later convicted in Bay County also and was sentenced to life in prison. The Florida Supreme Court overturned Ray's conviction, because, according to the record, Hall was the ringleader and received the lesser sentence.

There was another circuit court case that was in some regard sad, and yet humorous at the same time. A local man, McCants, was arrested for sexual battery. He was a Vietnam veteran who got a monthly check and had plenty of friends the first few days of each month. McCants was charged with the attempted rape of a woman. According to the testimony at the trial, the woman who made the allegation of rape was actually his girlfriend. McCants had served time in the state mental hospital previous to this event. Doctors had decided he was competent to stand trial.

During the trial the Bonifay police chief testified against McCants. As the chief was testifying, the defendant was sitting at the defense table, pointing at the chief as if his finger were a pistol. The judge reprimanded McCants several times. Finally the defendant interrupted the proceedings and pointed to the seal of the state of Florida that hung behind the judge. He asked the judge if he knew who the lady on the seal was. McCants was referring to the Indian maiden on the seal. The judge said to him, "Why don't you tell me." He said, "Judge, that Indian girl was Pocahontas, and she was kidnapped by the Spaniards and taken to Spain. When she returned some years later they had a big celebration and called it the Gasparilla Celebration." The seal of Florida actually has a Spanish galleon with an Indian girl in the foreground against what looks like a bay in the background. The judge never lost his composure; he just looked down and said, "Thank you, Mr. McCants, for the history lesson. Now you sit down or I am going to have the deputies sit you down." With that said he sat down beside his attorney, Russell Cole, the public defender. The trial was completed; McCants was convicted and sent to prison. He was later transferred to the mental facility in the state prison system. Whenever I see the seal of the state of Florida, I am reminded of McCants.

One of the most interesting hearings I ever attended involved the Woods brothers, William and Walter. The two of them had moved to Holmes County and were long haul truckers. Several times someone broke in their home while they were away. They decided that one of them would stay home when the other one left on the next trip and maybe they could find out who the perpetrators were. William Wood stayed behind, and sure enough, sometime after his brother had left, a couple of ruffians showed up. William confronted them before he found out for certain they were the culprits. He had a baseball bat and accused them of being the ones who had broken into their home. The boys denied it, but William commenced beating the truck they were driving. He broke out the windows and hit one of them before they could get away. They went to the sheriff's office and filed a complaint against William.

A deputy went out to William's home and arrested him for assault with a deadly weapon. William was appointed the public defender, Ed Ivey, who had at one time shared an office with the circuit judge, Russell Cole. William got out on bond but refused to make any appointments with the public defender. Ed Ivey finally got William and his brother to a hearing before Judge Cole, who was considering having William examined to determine his competence to stand trial.

The hearing started right after lunch, and William was not cooperating at all. The state attorney was Doug White, a very capable prosecutor. He told the judge he thought that Wood had been drinking. The judge asked him if he had been, and Wood said, "Yes, I have had six beers." His brother told the judge he had not had six beers; he'd only had one with his lunch. William spoke up and said, "They think I had six whatever I say, so I thought I would just say six right to start with." Wood then said to the judge, "I just want to know what kind of incestuous relationship you and Mr. Ivey have." Wood was referring to the fact that they had shared an office. The judge explained to William that he was going to have him evaluated. William replied, "Judge, I can save you the trouble, because I was in Vietnam and I am crazy as hell." The judge promptly told William that he too had been in Vietnam and that did not make him crazy. William was sent for evaluation, and he later skipped bond.

Some years later the social security administration called and informed me that William Wood was drawing social security. Since we still had a warrant for William, the law required them to tell us where he was. The agent said William was back in Kentucky and doing quite well. I called the sheriff's department and told them what had been reported. They said they had all the problems they needed and were not interested in having him back. Hopefully William found the happiness that eluded him in Holmes County.

One of the state attorney's best prosecutors, Doug White, had a couple of interesting cases in Holmes County. A police officer from Miami, who was originally from Holmes County, had come home to check on his aging father. The father had hired a Mexican farmhand to move into a mobile home on his property. The arrangement for some reason had not worked out to the satisfaction of the owner. He had asked the hand to get out of the mobile home. When the son came for a visit, the father told him about the tenant's slow progress in moving out. According to the complaint in the case file, the officer went over to the mobile home where the farmhand was living, with gun in hand, and banged on the door. He told the farmhand he had a short period of time to get out or he would be back. The tenant called the sheriff's department, and when a deputy arrived, the police officer was arrested for threatening the farmhand. The case progressed to a jury trial. Once the jury was seated, the state called the victim as its first witness. The courtroom had a large crowd present, which was unusual for this type of case. Several people in the audience were members of the Miami police department who had come to support their fellow officer.

As the victim began to tell his side of the story he recounted how scared he had been when someone banged on his door with a gun in his hand. He explained how he had called the sheriff's department and how the case had gotten to the point it was today. He then made a statement that Doug White pounced on. The victim told the court that he did not want to file charges; all he wanted was an apology. Doug then asked the victim, "What if the defendant apologized to you today, would that be sufficient?" The victim said, "Yes, it would." The prosecutor then asked the judge for permission to have a little, as he called it, "frontier justice," and have the defendant apologize in open court. The defendant did so with remorse in his voice, and the prosecutor then announced that the state would dismiss the case. The courtroom erupted with shouts of approval from the other police officers as the case concluded.

Doug also handled another interesting case in Holmes County. The case style was the *State of Florida v. Rory Moore.* Rory had been one of my 4-H boys when I was the 4-H coordinator for the county, before I entered politics. He had a girlfriend whose young child was rushed to the emergency room with bruises and internal injuries and later died. After an investigation, Rory was arrested and charged with being the one who had perpetrated the injuries on the child. A local attorney was hired to represent Rory, and the case went to trial. The state had a weak case, and as the witnesses testified, no one was able to point the finger at Rory, including the mother.

The first defense witness was a young boy who gave a riveting testimony. He said that he had attended a birthday party at the home of the defendant and his girlfriend. The young man testified further that as the party progressed, he went into a room where the deceased child was being held by his sister. He said all of a sudden the girl dropped the baby and then placed it back in the crib. The jury took very little time in finding him not guilty.

Through the years Interstate 10 has unfortunately brought Holmes County more than its share of criminal cases. One such case began when members of a Laotian gang stopped at a convenience store in Ponce de Leon, Florida. Several members of the gang waited in the car while one cased the place for possible criminal activities. A young black man from nearby Walton County happened to be in the store at the same time. The young man was wearing a gold chain. One of the Laotians tried to take the chain from him, and a fight ensued. A gang member pulled a gun and shot the young black man in the leg, striking an artery. The gang members escaped before law enforcement arrived. The young man died some time later in a Defuniak Spring, Florida, hospital.

Law enforcement made little progress solving the crime until the gang got into a shootout with some unsavory characters in a drug transaction in Mobile, Alabama. One of the gang members was shot, and his friends took him by a Mobile hospital and dumped him in the emergency room. He survived and later told Alabama investigators all about the shootings in Mobile and Holmes County. The gang members were brought back to Holmes County and charged. All but one pled and agreed to testify against the shooter. The shooter's trial was moved to Bay County because of all the pretrial publicity in Holmes County. He was found guilty and sentenced to life in prison for his crimes.

Sometimes court rulings seem almost irrational. One such case involved five inmates at the Homes Correction Institution in Bonifay. The five filed for name changes under Florida's easy-name-change law. The petitions plainly said the name changes were for religious purposes and that all the inmates had converted to Islam. They filed affidavits of indigence saying they had no money to file the civil cases. They wanted the local taxpayers to pay for their name changes. I did not think the county should have to pay for the name changes, so I sent the petitions back to them. They quickly filed for a writ of mandamus with the district court of appeals. It usually takes the appellant court months or years to decide a case for regular, law-abiding citizens. The prisoners got moved up the docket, and the court issued a notice to me to show cause in my official position as clerk. Gerald Holley, the county attorney at that time, filed my answer for me, basically stating the Constitution of the State of Florida and of the United States prohibited spending public funds for a religious purpose.

In a very short period of time the court ruled that my job was ministerial and that I was to file the petitions presented and let the circuit judge decide what to do with the cases. Two of my sons are attorneys, and at some time in their research they found this case. The prisoners won the battle but lost the war. Judge Cole would not allow the prisoners to be transported for civil hearings, and the five never got their names changed. I always felt that the name change had more to do with clearing their criminal record than for their newly found religious fervor.

Through the years we have had more than our share of drug cases. One of the largest drug cases in the county's history was called the Reedy Creek Ranch drug bust. A former deputy sheriff from a South Florida county bought the Reedy Creek Ranch in Holmes County from a local citizen. He, along with his wife and another individual, closed off public access to the ranch. They planted forty acres of corn and interspersed marijuana plants with the corn, thinking that the illegal plants would be hard to see. A Florida Highway Patrol plane working I-10 traffic control made a circle over their ranch and spotted the marijuana plants. The FHP notified the Holmes County sheriff's office. The sheriff's office made a raid and uncovered the largest marijuana field in county history. Along with the discovery came the arrest of the three "ranchers."

The three were tried in circuit court in Holmes County, and all were found guilty. When the trial was over the clerk's office had a large amount of marijuana that had been entered as evidence and only a small vault to store it.

During this same time period, another clerk in a much larger county in Florida resigned because her chief deputy's husband was arrested for replacing bales of marijuana with hay bales in her evidence vault. The incident was so embarrassing to the clerk that she retired before her term was over. After this incident, I went to the circuit judge and asked him for an order to have the marijuana destroyed. He gave me an order to have the drug plants burned. I took several witnesses, including a member of the press, to be sure there were no questions about what happened to the plants. The next day at the coffee shop someone told me that all the buzzards in the county had gathered at the county landfill and were high as a kite. We never kept large amounts of drugs in the clerk's evidence vault after that. The laws have changed since then, and law enforcement is required to keep only a sample of the drugs if there is a large quantity.

Holmes County had another infamous drug case involving the Tri-County Airport. The sheriff's department received information about a drug distribution group using the local airport. They set up a sting operation that caught the dealers landing a plane with drugs onboard. The sheriff's department made several arrests. That night, for some unknown reason, the sheriff's department left the plane unguarded, and someone from the drug ring returned to the airport in the middle of the night and flew the plane to Mexico. The sheriff's department was the object of many jokes over the next few weeks. One story told in the local coffee shop was that a local convenience store's huge chicken, advertising their famous fried chicken, now had around-the-clock protection from the sheriff's department. It was reported that the sheriff said the plane got away, but the darn chicken sure wouldn't!

The pilot of the plane was Chester McGraw. He was charged with drug trafficking, among other things. The Florida Department of Law Enforcement cut a deal with him to rejoin the drug ring he was working for and assist law enforcement with other arrests. The group took him back and offered to pay him as always. He called his FDLE handler and told them that he had been offered money. The agent told him to take the money. McGraw was smart enough to tape the conversation with the agent.

Later the agency wanted to renege on the deal they had made because he took the money. The state attorney's office brought McGraw before Holmes County judge Warren Edwards, who was then an acting circuit judge. The state told the judge that McGraw had broken his plea agreement by accepting the money and wanted him sentenced the full amount under the law. McGraw, acting as his own attorney, informed the court that an FDLE agent, had given him permission to take the money and that he had a tape to prove it. The state attorney objected and told the judge that if McGraw played the tape he would file additional charges against him for taping the conservation without telling the agent. The judge allowed the tape to be played, and it was just as the defendant said: He told the agent that the drug dealers were trying to pay him and he thought it would be suspicious if he refused to take the money. The agent clearly told him to go ahead. The judge told McGraw that even though the agent had told him it was all right, he had still violated his plea agreement. He was sentenced to the Florida Department of Corrections, but not for as long as the state had requested. McGraw got out of prison and was later killed in a plane crash in South Alabama. This closed one of the county's most embarrassing drug cases.

When I first became clerk there was a murder committed at the local county fair. In fact, for three years in a row someone connected to the carnival died while in Holmes County. All the deaths occurred under mysterious circumstances. One of the deaths resulted in the filing of charges against the son of the carnival owner. The case looked like an easy case to prosecute. There were two eye witnesses. The carnival owner hired Panama City attorney Fred Turner. He was the same attorney who represented Clarence Earl Gideon in his famous retrial. *Gideon v. Wainwright* was the case that established that a defendant in a criminal case was entitled to an attorney, even if he could not afford one. Turner, who later became circuit judge Fred Turner, did a masterful job of confusing the state's two eyewitnesses. The prosecutor in the case was Jim Appleman, who later was elected state attorney for the circuit. He laid out the state's case in a convincing manner, only to have Turner seat witnesses who put the young defendant in Port St. Joe at the time of the murder. It did not take the jury long to find the defendant not guilty.

The criminal cases that were the most difficult for me to cope with were the sexual abuse cases. Many times the abuse was perpetrated on the children of the accused. These cases have become more numerous over the years. Most of these crimes seem to be committed by people who moved in from another area to Holmes County and were actually apprehended here. The worst case I can remember involved a man who moved to the county and brought with him several children. A neighbor reported to authorities that his children were not attending school. An investigator from child services went to the home, and what they found was appalling. The children were all malnourished, and when they were taken out of the home the tales they told were horrifying. One son told of the father circumcising him on the kitchen table with the whole family, including the grandmother, watching. The father pled not guilty to the charges. We all had to sit through the trial and listen to the boy tell the horrifying stories of the abuse his father perpetrated against him and the others in the home. It did not take the jury long to find the father guilty. He was sentenced to life in prison.

There was another abuse case where a man was charged with abusing his own children. He was found guilty and sentenced to prison. The entire time he was in prison he bombarded the clerk's office with requests for information that would, according to him, prove his innocence. He appealed his case to the appellant court, and after they confirmed his conviction and entered a mandate, he continued to send demands to us. Judge Russell Cole finally issued an order that I was to receive no further filings from him. That solved the problem until he got out of prison and had access to a telephone. He started calling and harassing my deputy clerks day after day. One day he actually showed up in Bonifay persisting with his demands. One of my deputies alerted me to the fact that he was in the court department. I had to go back and deal with him. He began our conversation reasonably enough, but the new girlfriend he brought along became quite irate. Both of them began telling me that I was withholding information that would prove his innocence. It became apparent that there was no reasoning with them. I assured them there was no secret evidence being withheld and told them they should leave or I would call the sheriff. They left, threatening me as they went. I went home and told my wife to put the man on the list of suspects in case anything suspicious happened to me.

My oldest son, Zach, in addition to his private practice in Panama City, Florida works part time for the state attorney's office handling Jimmy Rice cases. The Jimmy Rice Statute in Florida is named after a young boy who was kidnapped and murdered by a pedophile. When a sexual offender has served their term in prison, they must be evaluated by a state psychiatrist to determine if they still pose a threat to minors. The offender can be sent to a state mental institute if they are found to be likely to reoffend. A jury trial is held in which a jury decides if the person is to be committed. Zach has been very successful in handling these cases, which are civil in nature. It also has given him an opportunity to keep his trial skills sharpened.

The most aggravating case I was ever involved in was one that occurred because I was trying to help someone. Florida law provides for a local canvassing board made up of the supervisor of elections, the chairman of the board of county commissioners, and the county judge. The county judge, by law, is the chairman of the canvassing board. The law says that if one of the members is running for office they cannot serve and the chief judge of the circuit can appoint someone to replace them. Years ago, when Judge Brown was opposed, he asked if I would take his place on the canvassing board. The election came and went, and there were no problems.

As time went on the judge routinely asked me to take his place whether he was running or not, and I always agreed. I actually enjoyed the task, which included counting the absentee votes. One year we were counting the absentee votes, and we discovered that several voters had written in names for different offices. Florida law allows voters to write in a name if they choose. The count was being conducted during a presidential election, and someone wrote my name in for president. I was feeling really important because I got a vote for the highest office in the land. In a few minutes, however, we counted another write-in vote for president, Mickey Mouse. Mickey later got one more vote, and the important feeling I had quickly dissipated, since Mickey beat me two to one.

The judge once again asked me to take his place on the board for the 2000 elections. The chief judge signed an order to that effect. John Braxton, who had retired as sheriff after several terms, decided that he did not like being retired and decided to run against the man who had replaced him, Dennis Lee. The canvassing board was made up of Rick Crews, the chairman of the county commission; Debbie Wilcox Morris, the supervisor of elections; and me.

Election Day was no problem. We went through the tasks that were required by the law. There were several hundred absentee ballots that had to be counted, and part of our duty was to check some of the signatures to make sure they matched the ones on record. The supervisor's staff had already verified most of the signatures but had left approximately fifty or so ballots for the board to decide on. It had always been my theory that every vote that could be reasonably ascertained to be signed by the voter should be counted. As we went through the stack of ballots, some were obviously not signed by the person who had signed the voter registration document on file in the supervisor's office. The most obvious discrepancy I remember was the signature of a lady who signed her registration with an *X*, and her ballot was signed very nicely in cursive handwriting. We went through the ballots and counted all the ones that we could match with their signatures on file. There were twenty-five ballots that we did not count. The absentee ballots are processed during the day on Election Day and then fed into the machine but not totaled until after the polls closed that night.

That night, as the precincts' numbers began to come in, we could see the sheriff's race was going to be close. Braxton stayed just a few votes ahead until one of the last precincts came in. When Poplar Springs School precinct reported, Lee went ahead. Lee was up by five votes when the final votes were counted. We had a great number of people on both sides present, trying to help us count. The board decided that we would meet the first thing in the morning and do the mandatory recount that is required. The Holmes

County sheriff's race was the least of our worries. During the night the presidential election came down to just a few hundred votes in Florida, and the secretary of state ordered all the canvassing boards in the state to also do a presidential recount.

When we got to the courthouse the next morning we were not only met with the sheriff candidates and their supporters but also news media and lawyers from each of the parties wanting to see the presidential recount. We started the dual recount of the sheriff's race and the president's at the same time. After the recount, the sheriff's race stayed the same, with Braxton picking up maybe one vote. Bush picked up a few votes in the presidential race. The crowds had begun to get a little restless, with some folks on the Braxton side demanding a manual recount. Things were getting pretty hot when a local attorney representing the Republican Party came up to me. He asked me why I was down there taking all the heat for the county judge, who was getting paid to do the job. He said I needed to look at the order that appointed me.

I called for a recess, went to my office, and found the order where the chief judge had appointed me to the canvassing board. The wording was for the primaries only. The general election was not included on the order. I thought the Lord had delivered me again. When I called the chief judge and explained the problem, she offered to do an updated order. I told her I had no problem doing the job I was elected to do but I would not agree to the amended order. She said, "I do not blame you." At that point she called Judge Brown and apprised him of the situation. He came down and replaced me on the canvassing board.

The canvassing board, after finishing the recount, certified Dennis Lee the winner in the sheriff's race by five votes and also certified the votes in the presidential election. Shortly thereafter the losing sheriff candidate filed a lawsuit against the canvassing board. Not only was there a civil suit, but some citizens asked the governor to investigate the matter as a criminal case. The governor appointed state attorney Willie Meggs to do a criminal investigation. Former sheriff Braxton's suit challenged the election, the recount, and the twenty-five absentees that the canvassing board had thrown out. The case was first assigned to circuit judge Clinton Foster and later to senior judge Michael Miller. Judge Miller held several hearings and finally ruled that the plaintiffs had failed to prove fraud on the part of the canvassing board and that the results, with Lee as winner, would stand. Braxton appealed to the district court of appeals, and after five years the appellant court upheld Judge Miller but ordered him to look at the twenty-five absentees. The case was sent back. Judge Miller opened the ballots, looked at them, and announced that his opinion still stood. He resealed the twenty-five ballots.

As the civil case progressed slowly through the court system, the Leon County state attorney's office conducted the criminal investigation. The investigator came to Holmes County, looked at all the records, and concluded there were no criminal violations. The state attorney withheld his final report until the disposition of the civil case. (See appendix A.)

This was a very trying time for all of us involved. The attorney for Braxton went out of her way attempting to intimidate all of us by taking our depositions and asking all kinds of personal questions. She asked me if the sheriff had furnished me a gun; apparently he had loaned one to Judge Brown. She asked me if I knew the definition of an under vote. I thought a long time before I answered, and I said, "Yes, I do know the definition of an under vote; it's the opposite of an over vote." The courtroom erupted with laughter. The attorney, in her signature nasal tone, sarcastically said, "All right,

Mr. Taylor, so much for your humor." She then asked the judge to make me answer. The judge told her that I had answered. At that time I did go on and explain the difference. She asked Judge Brown to list the different kinds of medications he was taking and if he thought that they impaired his ability to think clearly. The judge said he did not think they did.

While I served on the canvassing board, neither of the other board members ever indicated who their preference for sheriff was. Judge Miller made it clear that nothing less than proof of fraud on the part of the canvassing board would result in overturning the election results as certified by the board.

Prior to her taking office as supervisor of elections Debbie Morris had worked for me in the clerk's office. I knew firsthand that she was very competent in the performance of her duties as required by Florida law. Seeing her honesty and integrity questioned seemed unfair. Therisa Meadows, one of her deputy supervisors, had also worked for me as a bookkeeper. She possessed the same standard of honesty. It was a relief for all involved when the state attorney, appointed by the governor, returned his finding after the civil suit was settled. His report to the governor listed no criminal findings. The filing of this report effectively ended all the legal activity involved in this case.

As more people moved into the county there are more landline disputes now than there were years ago. Newcomers buy a little parcel of land, have it surveyed, and think they own the world. They start telling the neighbors where to move their fences to accommodate their survey. The newcomers, instead of making friends with their new neighbors, start feuds that persist for long periods of time. I always tell people when they come to see me about their landline dispute, that it can be settled in one of three ways. Number one, they can leave the fence or line where it is. Number two, they can move the fence to a point they both can agree on. Number three, hire a lawyer, file a petition in court, and let the court tell them where the line is. Too many times the people have taken the last option, and after the loss of a great deal of time and money they still are not happy, and sometimes they're even less happy than before.

One particular landline dispute that comes to mind ended in 2010. The people on one side came to see me and talked to me about the case. I told them the usual options about settling the case they asked for a recommendation for a good landline attorney. I told them my pick would be Gerald Holley from Chipley, who to my knowledge had not lost a landline case in Holmes County. They hired Gerald, and he filed the suit. The other side hired an attorney from Jackson County, Florida, and the case lingered for a couple of years in the court system. The attorney from Jackson County withdrew from the case, and the defendant hired my son Luke as his attorney. So the plaintiff had the attorney I recommended, and the defendant had my son as his attorney. The trial was held in February of 2010. Judge Register placed the line in dispute somewhere in between where each landowner wanted it.

We had a very interesting personal injury case filed several years ago. There is an intersection north of Ponce de Leon where State Road 81 and County Road 181 meet. This intersection was the scene of an accident between a truck and a motorcycle. A student, going to school at Ponce de Leon High School, pulled out from the east side of County Road 181 and headed south toward the school. A county school bus driven by Eugene Holmes was stopped on the west side of County Road 181 getting ready to turn south toward Ponce de Leon High School. A motorcycle operated by the plaintiff was traveling south on State Road 81 toward Ponce de Leon.

It was a foggy day with low visibility. The student driver testified that he looked both ways before turning south and did not see any vehicles. There was a car ahead of the motorcycle just north of the intersection. The motorcycle driver began passing the southbound vehicle at the same time that the student in the truck turned south onto Highway 81. The motorcycle operator realized he was going to hit the truck that had pulled out. He tried to avoid the truck but caught the right rear bumper, resulting in him being thrown over the truck onto the shoulder of the highway. He sustained injuries, but they were not life threatening.

During the trial the defense attorney called Eugene Holmes, the bus driver, as a witness. He asked Eugene to testify, using a diagram, to establish where the motorcycle passed the car before it collided with the truck. Eugene showed the lawyer and the jury on the diagram where he saw the motorcycle pass the car. The lawyer began to try to get Eugene to change his story to say the motorcycle passed the car farther down the road. The lawyer kept pressing Eugene and finally said, "Mr. Holmes is it possible that the motorcycle might have passed the car farther down the road than where you indicated?" Eugene, having become pretty upset by this time, answered emphatically, "No, it's not possible, because if he did, he would have passed him twice!" The whole courtroom, including the jury, erupted in laughter. The lawyer quietly sat down, realizing he had asked Eugene one question too many.

There was another civil suit that I was reluctantly drawn into involving an elderly man and his relatives. The man lived on a small farm in the county. He had one child, a daughter, who lived in another area. The man was cared for by a nephew who lived nearby. It was understood throughout the community that the nephew would inherit the elderly man's property at the time of his death, but no paperwork to that effect was ever prepared. The man's daughter came home one day and took her father down to the courthouse to the property appraiser's office to have a deed prepared giving his property to her. Jack Faircloth, the property appraiser at that time, was related to the man and his daughter, so he thought nothing of complying with the man's request. The deed was signed in the tax collector's office and notarized by the employees who worked there. At the time of the man's death, the nephew realized that the daughter had a deed to the land. He hired a local attorney and filed a suit to set the deed aside. The case was then assigned to a circuit judge, Judge John Roberts.

The final hearing was held in the courthouse in Bonifay. Jack Faircloth, the employees of the tax collector's office, and I were all called as witnesses. The defendant's attorney called me to see if I knew anything about the deed being signed or about the recording. I knew nothing of the deed being prepared or signed. All I could testify to was what was recorded in the public records. Jack Faircloth was really the witness whose testimony decided the case. He said the old man came to his office and requested him to prepare the deed, which he did. He then sent the man to the tax collector's office to have the deed notarized and witnessed. The tax collector's employees confirmed what Jack had said. After each side presented closing arguments, Judge Roberts told the attorneys he was ready to give his decision. Most judges, seeing a heavily stacked courtroom, supporting the plaintiffs, would have taken the case under advisement and rendered their decision at a later date. Judge Roberts, however, announced that he ruled for the defendant. He said he was convinced that the man had signed the deed willingly and intended for his daughter to have the land.

The most expensive civil case the county has ever been involved in was the landfill case. The county had operated garbage dumps throughout the area for many years. The Florida Department of

Environmental Protection (DEP) decided that the dumps were a threat to the environment and ordered them closed. The county hired an engineer to design a modern facility that would enable the county to continue the garbage disposal business. The county closed all the dumps as directed and obtained the land for one eighty-three-acre central landfill. It was permitted, and the county successfully ran it for many years. Then DEP increased regulations to run a landfill, and the county began to have trouble meeting the standards. Some of the new requirements involved placing plastic liners in each of the cells before the garbage could be put in. Another requirement required the monitoring of wells. When the county applied for a new operating permit, DEP would not issue it. They wanted the county to make major upgrades to the facility or close it. The commissioner who was sent by the county to meet with DEP regarding the problems basically told DEP where to go and left the meeting with nothing settled. DEP countered with a recommended consent order that required the county to close the landfill by a certain date.

Meanwhile, an attorney from Jackson County had formed a company and was interested in getting into the garbage disposal business. He approached the board and told them that his company would purchase the landfill and deal with DEP to keep the site going as a private operation. Basically the county would not have any liability in the closure or in running the operation. The board, at the time, was split on accepting the offer. After some time the board did accept his offer on a four-to-one vote. The board agreed to the eighty-three-acre landfill, but when the contract approved by the board was returned, there were 720 additional acres added to the original description, making the new site over 800 acres. The group that had purchased the landfill from the county immediately started trying to flip the operation to a large national garbage disposal company and in fact did get an agreement to sell to City Environmental. Word of the big regional landfill began to get out in the county, and a group formed opposing the idea. Many citizens did not like the idea of garbage being hauled to the county from other counties.

The issue simmered and reached a boiling point when City Environmental applied for a land-use permit to expand the landfill to the adjoining 720 acres. The county commissioners had to approve the land-use change, and the political heat began to increase. Most of the board seemed to support the eighty-three-acre site, but City Environmental said it could not economically operate on such a small site and needed the larger acreage. When the county commission would not approve the larger landfill, City Environmental sued the county in federal court and state court. The suit in federal court was filed to invalidate the county ordinance that prohibited bringing garbage into Holmes County from other counties. They also sued in state court for breach of contract. The county attorney was Gerald Holley, a competent county lawyer but one who did not like to practice in federal court. I suggested to Mr. Holley that he recommend Tom Pelham to the board. Tom was a Holmes County native who had served as the secretary of community affairs under Governor Bob Martinez. He was well acquainted with the complex issues involved. When he was hired he asked the board to allow him to retain another Tallahassee attorney, Larry Simpson, to handle the federal case. Simpson was a former prosecutor, best known for putting serial killer Ted Bundy on death row.

The City Environmental lawyers were a group of attorneys from Detroit who were totally out of their element in Holmes County. One of them jokingly asked after the first hearing was over if anyone could tell him where the American Embassy was. It was clear from the start that the county had the best legal team. Pelham and

Simpson were terrific together and began to pick apart the case that had been filed. The only setback from a legal standpoint came early in the case when the federal judge struck down the county ordinance that prohibited garbage from being brought in from other counties. The judge said under the commerce clause of the US Constitution, only Congress could regulate this activity. The county's attorneys had already told the board they would lose this issue, so it was not a surprise.

With the federal suit out of the way, the issues of the state case began to come forward. City Environmental contended that the county commission knew from the start that the new landfill would be eight hundred acres, not eighty-three. The county countered that the attachment that included the additional land was added after the agreement left the county and that there was never a meeting of the minds, a requirement under Florida law. The attorney who had obtained the original contract from the county was deposed in the case. He testified that I carried the county seal from the courthouse out to the business of Wayne Marsh, who was the chairman of the board at the time. He testified that Mr. Marsh signed the contract in my presence and I signed and sealed the document, which included the additional acreage. Thank goodness Mr. Marsh told the truth and said I had never been in his business with the county seal. I of course affirmed his testimony, since I had never taken the county seal out of the courthouse.

The trial was moved to Panama City at the request of the plaintiffs, because they did not think they could get a fair trial in Holmes County. I was one of the first witnesses to be called, and the attorney tried to confuse me about the board's intention concerning the additional 720 acres. The trial lasted about a week, and in the end, the jury ruled in favor of the county.

The story does not end there, however. A large national company bought City Environmental and all the rights to the Holmes County landfill. A man who purported to be a representative of the new company contacted the county commission. He told the board that his company wanted to sign any right they had on the eight-three acres back to the county. He said they would help the county get the money from the Florida legislature to close the landfill under the DEP consent order.

The legislative session had already started, and I called our state senator to verify that the money was in the budget. The senator's aide told me that no one had contacted the senator about any money for the county. He said the $850,000 that we had been promised was not going to get funded because it was too late in the session. I relayed the information to the board, and it appeared the board had been contacted by some scam artist. About a week later I got a call from the senator's office informing me that the county had $850,000 in the DEP budget for landfill closure. The county was instructed to hire a contractor from Louisiana to perform the closure. The county was informed they would do the job for an amount less than the $850,000, and the county was allowed to use the rest of the money to satisfy DEP consent order items at the site. The national company delivered the deed to the county for the eighty-three acres. This whole process seemed a little strange. The man from the national company was better informed than we gave him credit for being. He apparently knew how the system worked and how to get things done.

The citizens group that had been fighting to keep the landfill out of the county had demanded that the high-rise cell that had been built at the landfill site be moved. This issue was holding up the final settlement of the case, which the county had won at trial. The mystery man, the representative from the company, came back on the scene to tell the county that DEP would not approve moving the high-rise cell. Sure enough, within a couple of days a letter came from DEP informing the county that they could not remove the high-rise cell. A short time later the Florida legislature appropriated the $850,000 to close the landfill. The county commissioners awarded the contract to Heber E. Costello of Oak Grove, Louisiana, for $583,000. The company brought its crew to Holmes County and shortly completed the closure. The landfill issue that had been so costly was finally over.

Both the attorneys told me that the records that we kept in the clerk's office were instrumental in helping the county prevail in the case by providing true and accurate information for the jury. It reminded me of a Harry Truman story. He was on his famous train campaign stop. He stopped to give a speech, and someone in the crowd yelled, "Give 'em hell, Harry!" Harry responded to the man by saying, "I never give 'em hell; I just tell the truth and they think its hell." [ii]

There was another federal suit filed against the county involving Americans with Disabilities complaints. An individual sued the county, the school board, and the city of Bonifay, along with all the restaurants in town, over lack of ADA compliance. The county was able to settle the complaint for a small amount. All the buildings were rightly brought into full ADA compliance.

Several years prior to the suit, a lady contacted the county commission about the courthouse not having an elevator. The board did not take any action at that time. I contacted State Representative Durelle Peaden to ask if he would put in a budget request for the county to install an elevator in the courthouse. He put in the request, and it was funded. The contract was awarded, and the elevator, handicap bathrooms, and handicap parking were all done with the state money. I called the lady who had brought the issue to the board and asked if she would come down and cut the ribbon for the new elevator. She was pleased to, and I thanked her for reminding us of our obligations to the citizens in our county who needed the accommodations. Having the elevator has made a big difference not only for handicapped citizens but also for the deputy clerks who have to take loaded file carts to and from court.

Restraining Orders

One of the saddest and most aggravating parts of the clerk's job is dealing with domestic violence restraining orders. Domestic violence is a serious problem, and we handled each case carefully with that in mind. Many of the injunctions that people applied for were dismissed before the hearing. Deputy clerks did a great job preparing the paperwork to present to the judge but often got caught in the crossfire. Many times I was called to the court department to get between the husband and wife or girlfriend and boyfriend. People wanted to fight custody and impending divorce battles through restraining orders. Everyone in the judicial system operated on the "cover your behind" theory. I told my deputy clerks to help process the paperwork regardless of how trivial the event seemed—just send it on to the judge and let him sort out the mess. Judges were not pleased sometimes because the events did not qualify and they thought we should not have filed the case.

In a small county like ours, it was not uncommon for me to know both parties involved in an injunction. One lady came in and told me that her husband had threatened to kill her and she wanted an injunction against him. We filled out the paperwork, and the judge signed the order. That night my wife and I were eating in a local restaurant, and sitting across from us was the man and woman who had obtained the injunction. They spoke to me just like nothing had happened. Another thing some people do not realize is that the injunction is temporary. A final hearing will be held within ten days, with the other party receiving notice to be present. At this time, the other party may tell their side of the story. After the judge has a final hearing he or she decides whether to make the injunction permanent or dismiss the complaint.

CHILD SUPPORT JUDGMENTS

The Florida legislature enacted a law several years ago requiring clerks of court in the state to implement a new process where the clerk would record a judgment against any person who was late on child support. The law required the clerk to keep a record of all court-ordered child support. When the payor was fifteen days late, a notice was sent informing the person they were late with their child support. The notice told them a judgment would be recorded against them if they did not pay within fifteen days. This judgment was the only judgment that could be signed by the clerk and did not require the signature of a judge, as was the common practice. The judgment was called a judgment by operation of law. This meant that the amount could increase each time a payment was missed, without notification of the payor. Clerks resisted the implementation of this law because it put them in the awkward position of signing a judgment instead of having a judge sign it. A district court of appeals upheld the law. This appeals court opinion was a precedent that applied to all the clerks in Florida. Reluctantly, most clerks in the state, including me, took steps to apply the law.

We began sending out the notices, and many paid. Many did not, however, which left a high percentage of our child support cases with judgments. Through the years many people have been upset with me when I signed the judgment against them because they were behind on their child support. At the same time there were many happy when the judgment forced the debtor to pay the child support. Title companies were required to check to make sure that there were no child support judgments before they could sign off on any loan closing. Workman's compensation claims, Internal Revenue Service refunds, and lotto winnings could not be paid before the child support judgments were satisfied.

One day one of my deputy clerks told me that Gator Jones had gotten a worker's comp settlement and that he owed a child support balance. The insurance company wanted to send us the money to pay off the balance. I told the deputy to line up the ex-wife and Mr. Jones to come in to sign off on the settlement agreement and satisfaction before we disbursed the money. They both showed up and signed the paperwork, and we gave her the money. Gator looked at his ex-wife and told her, "I am glad to heck to be rid of you." He then turned to me and said, "And I am glad to heck to be rid of you." I probably should not have, but the only response for me seemed to be, "Yes, Gator, and I am glad to heck to be rid of you." The next time I saw Gator, he greeted me like we had never had the exchange.

The Florida child support collection, which is run cooperatively with the Florida Department of Revenue and the Florida Association of Court Clerks, is one of the most successful in the country. Millions of dollars in child support are collected each year for deserving children, and the clerks of Florida are a vital part of the process.

* * *

State Champs '66-'67

Bottom:L-R, Johnnie Sawyer, Alan Lane, Benny Joe Bell, Donnie Johnson;
Top:Ronnie Johnson,Cody Taylor, Doyle Holland, Gerald Hayes, Richard Kelly

1966 State Champs

Ronnie Yeomans, Dewitt Scott, Milton Burdeshaw, Donnie Johnson, Cody Taylor, Hilton Creel, Doyle Holland, Ronnie Johnson, Charles Burdeshaw, Benny Joe Bell, Hilton McSwain, and Gerald Hayes.

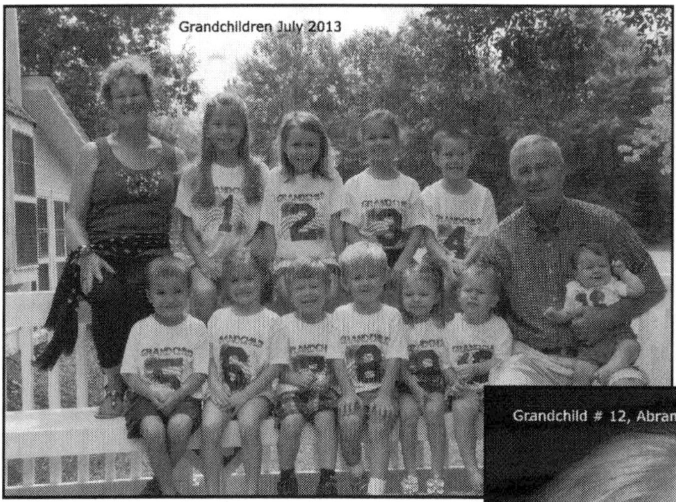
Grandchildren July 2013

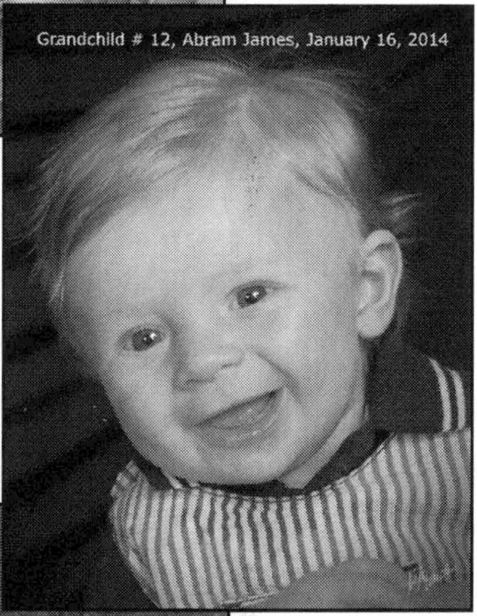
Grandchild # 12, Abram James, January 16, 2014

Taylor Family July 2013

senior 1967

second grade

Deputy Clerks
L-R: Beth West, Chris Forehand, Cindy Jackson, Frankie Short, Karin Bridger, Alice Vickers, Jennifer Ellenburg,Kathy Lee, Diane Eaton, Angie Purvee, Elizabeth Arnold, (not pictured, Angie Jonas, Bethany Riley)

Holmes County Clerks left to right Judge Helms, 20 years, Cody Taylor, 36 years, and Jack Faircloth, 8 years

CHAPTER 5

County Auditor and Recorder

County Commissioners

During my thirty-six years in office, I served with over thirty county commissioners. Some of them were the most honest and straightforward men I have ever known. Most made decisions based on what they deemed to be the best interest of the county. Watching how the members handled controversy and hard economic times was always interesting to me. Most years I would spend hours with the board in budget hearings, trying to balance the county budget. After much effort the board would always get the job done. I will always remember former commissioner Jerry English in these times. He could find humor in every situation regardless of how bleak the future looked. His quiet, humorous, and thoughtful personality got the board through some rough times. Every board needs someone like him. I also saw many county commissioners become real decision makers during these workshops. These hard times called for a resourcefulness and creativity that was out of the ordinary realm of operation. They were forced to look at options and alternatives that might not have originally been within their optimum lists of solutions. Being a commissioner in a rural county with a small tax base is never an easy job.

The backgrounds of commissioners have always been interesting. Many times they have more in common than meets the eye. I was attending a commission meeting one day, and there was no one there but the five commissioners and me. The commissioners began to talk about their family backgrounds and discuss bootlegging, which of course is the illegal manufacture, sale, or distribution of alcohol. Before the meeting was over each of them admitted that someone in their family or someone they knew had taken part in some phase of bootlegging. Times were hard during the depression, and it was not easy to make a living. The county remained dry for many years, but finally a majority of the county citizens wanted to make the county wet, thus allowing the sale of alcohol and cutting the bootleggers out. The old-timers said it was the first they could remember that the church folks and the bootleggers were on the same side and voted together against the legal sale of alcohol.

Roads, Roads, and More Roads

County commissioners had an ongoing program to try to improve the roads of the county. As clerk I was constantly working to get state or federal help to fund paving or resurfacing projects. The first road I helped get paved was the extension of C-173 from State Road 2 to the Alabama state line. It was a missing link for many folks going to Dothan, Slocomb, or Hartford, Alabama. John Clark was the commissioner in that district in 1977. He and I discussed applying for a state grant to help with the road. The county would have to add some dollars for a match, but we were able to get a grant to pay for most of the road. Coggin and Dearmont Construction Company from Chipley, Florida, was the low bidder and received the contract to build the road.

The one stipulation for the citizens that owned land along the road was that the right of way would have to be donated, since the county did not have the money to buy it. Clyde Brown, a well-known lawyer, owned a tract of land in the Poplar Springs community. He suggested to me and the county commission that we have a meeting of all landowners at the Poplar Springs High School. The board set the meeting, and the county engineer presented the plans. During the discussion some thought the right of way was too wide and some thought it should be moved one way or the other. The discussion went on for some time, until all of a sudden Clyde Brown took the floor. He told the landowners that he had wanted this road paved for his entire lifetime. He stated emphatically that he had heard enough and if everyone else wanted to spend the night discussing the project that would be fine with him. He turned to me and said, "Cody, you got my deed ready for me to sign?" I told him I did. He signed the deed, and I notarized it. Everyone in the room got in line behind him and signed their deed without another question. In 2013 Highway 173 was widened and resurfaced from the Washington County line to the Alabama line. This was a much needed project that made possible a safer drive for the citizens who traveled it.

Another road that I was instrumental in getting paved was County Road 160 from State Road 79 to County Road 173. The county had financed a bond issue, and each commissioner got a set amount of money for his district. Gene Sims was the commissioner of this district and decided to use part of his money to do this project. He asked me to help him with the right of way. I contacted each of the landowners, and they all agreed, with the exception of one man. Commissioner Sims went with me to see the man about the right of way. He owned the first parcel, forty acres long, leaving State Road 79 going east. We met with him, and he was about to agree to give the right of way when his son came over. He reminded his dad that his wife did not want to give the right of way. The man backed out and told Gene it would take $3,000 to get his portion of the right of way.

On the way back to town Gene asked me what I thought we ought to do. I told him I would let the engineer advertise the road two ways. One alternative stopped the road forty acres short of Highway 79, and the other option finished the road. The road was advertised as I suggested and awarded on that basis. The landowner was stubborn and held out. One day I suggested to Gene that we should go ahead and pay the owner the money. I told him that ten years from now people would want to know what idiots had paved a road and left 1,320 feet as a dirt road. He reluctantly took the issue to the board. They agreed to buy the right of way in time for the contractor to finish the road all at once.

Many of the roads in Holmes County, as well as some in other small counties, would never have been paved if it had not been for some of the government grant programs. Several roads in Holmes County were paved with Community Development Block Grants. These grants would usually include some housing rehabilitation and road improvements. Padgett Farm Road, Gritney Road, and the Noma-Esto Road were examples of CDBG roads in the county.

The Florida legislature, with some heavy prodding from small county clerks and commissioners, also started putting some money in the state budget to help small counties with resurfacing. The state programs were the only revenue that most small counties had to keep paved roads upgraded and resurfaced.

Holmes County road 177, 177-A, 160, Son-in-Law Road, 171, 181, 185, 81-A, 10-A, 183-A, 179, 179-A and, 173 were all under these two programs. Road conditions in Holmes County are significantly better because it qualified for these programs.

Cody Taylor Lane

When the 911 program was installed in Holmes County the board of county commissioners had to decide whether to name all the roads or number them. The board at the time took the easy way out and put it on a referendum, which allowed the voters of the county to decide. I personally favored numbering, since I knew that it would be less expensive for the county. The vote was very close, with naming winning over numbering by less than ten votes. Before it was over, the board and the public wished that the numbering of the roads had won. Road names are hard for neighbors to agree on. There were constant arguments about who had lived there the longest. One lady went to a commissioner and said God told her to come and get him to change the name of one county road. She told him to name the road after her deceased husband. The commissioner informed her that when God told him that it needed to be changed, he would bring it up to the board. She came to a commission meeting and told the whole board what God revealed to her about the road. The board voted three to two to name the road after her deceased husband. The commissioner who served the district where the road was located voted against changing the name but was outvoted.

That brings me to Cody Taylor Lane. Some people think I named a road for myself; the truth of the matter is that the men at the county road department named it after me because Brenda and I were the first ones to live on the road. When the roads were named in our commission district, Cody Taylor Lane was added. I honestly did not know about the naming until the map was published. I guess I should just take credit for having named a road for myself, because that is what some people believe anyway.

GUARDING THE CHECKBOOK

The clerk of the circuit court is the guardian of the county's checkbook. Along with the checkbook, the clerk has several responsibilities under Florida law. Each bill has to be pre-audited by the clerk's office to make sure that the bill is a legal claim against the county. One thing clerks have to remember is that they cannot override a poor decision by the board to spend money. The clerk's responsibility is to make sure it is a legal expenditure. Through the years I have had to question many bills that came to the clerk's office and actually refused to pay many of them. The following are some of the ones that stand out in my mind.

The county was required by federal and state law to pay a portion of the county's Medicaid billing for county citizens who were on the Medicaid program. These billings were for hospital and nursing-home care. The Medicaid billing in Florida was done by a state agency that started billing the county an estimated total amount for patient care and expected me to pay the bill. I refused, as did several other clerks, and the department filed an administrative action against the county. I put the contested money in escrow, and the case proceeded. The county attorney at the time, Gerald Holley, sent the department a set of interrogatories asking for a great deal of information that the department could not provide. The department was in the middle of changing computer systems and apparently had lost much of the information and was unable to establish what each county owed. In desperation the department finally asked the county attorney if we would be willing to settle if they reduced the sum $90,000. The state finally got the new system up and running, so we settled the action and paid what we owed less the $90,000. The fact that we refused to pay an *estimated* bill saved the county a great deal of money.

Failure to get a change order involving road construction resulted in my refusing to pay another bill submitted to the county. The county signed an agreement to use the funds on a particular road for resurfacing only. The commissioner for the district and the engineer realized that there was going to be an overage of funds upon competition of the project. So without getting board approval they decided to instruct the contractor to pave a portion of a dirt road that led to a community church off the project road. The contractor knew he was supposed to get a change order. It was brought to my attention, and I told the board I would not sign the check unless they did a change order and got Florida Department of Transportation to approve it. The board decided not to approve the change order, and that left the contractor holding the bag so to speak. A meeting between the county attorney, the engineer, and the contractor did not produce a settlement, so the contractor had to eat the $25,000 bill.

I was fortunate to have good employees in the clerk's bookkeeping department. They consistently scrutinized bills that came to the county to determine if they were legitimate. It is the clerk's responsibility to make sure the board of commissioners budget is monitored through the expenditure process. It was a constant battle to get some department heads to obtain purchase orders and follow other sound accounting practices. The clerk's office received good audits through the years, showing all the money was accounted for.

There have been many natural disaster declarations that resulted in the county getting large amounts of federal and state funds to clean up after hurricanes and floods. There were so many storms during one period that we could not get one disaster closed before another one started. The county let several contracts to private contractors, and one contractor had bid a certain size loader. After the contract was awarded it was brought to my attention that the loader was not the size that he had bid. I asked Joey Marsh, the county's public works coordinator, to go out and measure the bucket on the loader, and it was a half yard short. I told the commissioner in that district of the overbilling. The total amount that was overbilled was $17,500. The next day, when the contractor and the commissioner came to see me, I presented the bill to the contractor, and he was upset. The Lord seemed to give me the right words to say at the right time. I told the man and the commissioner that an error in billings that was corrected probably was not a crime but fraudulent billing certainly was. The man took out his checkbook and wrote a check for $7,500 and withdrew the $10,000 bill that he had submitted, making the $17,500 credit. From that point the contractor billed all FEMA work at the smaller bucket size.

One county commissioner, during his one term of service, reminded me of a preacher my FFA teacher told us about in class one day. He said there was an old country church that had service once a month with a circuit-riding preacher. On a particularly hot August Sunday the traveling preacher arrived on his chosen mode of transportation, a donkey. He tied his donkey by the open well in front of the church, went in, and preached a sermon of over two hours. When he finally finished preaching he walked out and tried to jump up on the donkey, but he missed and fell in the well. One of the elderly deacons who had an opinion on every issue walked out the front door of the church and was heard saying, "I could have told you that fellow did not know his ass from a hole in the ground. Thank goodness this commissioner only served one term.

COUNTY RECORDER

The county recording department is an office that is operated on the fees collected for documents recorded. If filing fees are not sufficient to run the department the board of commissioners makes up the difference. If there is money left at the end of the year the excess goes to the county general fund.

The recording department records all documents relating to real estate including deeds, mortgages, and judgments in what is called official records. All final judgments in all civil cases are also recorded in the official records. Information on tax liens by the IRS and other agencies is also filed in the clerk's office. All deeds recorded in Florida are public records, and anyone can review the records or get a copy of anyone's deeds. On several occasions people would call and jump on me for giving their neighbor a copy of their deed. I would kindly tell them that first of all, I did not give the neighbor a copy; they paid one dollar per page. I would tell them I would be glad to sell them a copy of the other person's deed for the same amount. They would usually calm down and say something to the effect of "a person's deed should be private." Florida law now requires that official records be available for viewing on the Internet. The Holmes County clerk's office, through Clericus, now has over thirty years of official records on the web. Private information such as social security number, financial information or telephone number is redacted to protect the privacy of people who have recorded documents. The redaction is handled automatically by Clericus.

There is nothing like the courthouse burning to let people how important record security is. The Holmes County courthouse burned in the early 1900's along with most of the county records. People mentioned that to me when I ran for office and one of the first actions I took was to get approval from the county commission to microfilm all the records. A copy of all records was stored in an underground vault for security.

As technology improved many counties went fully digital and have no paper record for backup. Even though we went digital I made the decision that as long as I was clerk I would keep a paper copy for backup just in case.

Citizens of the county and particularly senior citizens have learned to depend on the clerk's office for the security of their important papers. I wanted to make sure that their confidence in me was not ill founded.

* * *

CHAPTER 6

CEREMONIES

MARRYING

Through the years I have married over 750 couples. I never wanted to marry anyone, but the law allows the clerk to perform the ceremony, so I got into the marrying business, with some reservations. I tried to get the first couple who came to me to go to a preacher because I thought that's what everyone wanted. I quickly learned that was not true, so I decided to do my legal duty. Judge Hutchinson loaned me a standard ceremony, and that is the one I used through the years unless the couple had one they wanted to use.

I have married people at my house, at their house, on the steps of the courthouse, and at the mansion at Point Washington where the movie *Frogs* was filmed. A fellow called me one time and asked me to perform the ceremony for his daughter on a Saturday afternoon, and I agreed. One of my boys had a little league game that lasted longer than it was supposed to, and I was late for the wedding. When I got to the house everyone was partying and having a wonderful time. I walked up, and the guy met me. He said, "Don't worry about being late; we just moved the reception up and now we can have the wedding."

Another time, three sailors from Jacksonville were on the way through Bonifay on I-10 and stopped to ask where they could get a marriage license. They were given my number, so I went down to the courthouse, issued the licenses, and married them all at one time. Brenda and the children were witnesses. I never heard from them and have no idea how long the marriages lasted.

Speaking of lasting, not all my marriage ceremonies held together all that long. I married one couple on a Friday, and the guy called me on Sunday and asked me if we would just tear up the licenses and forget the whole thing. I told him no, he would have to get a divorce.

Another man, whose name I will not divulge, had many short-lived marriages. After his last divorce I saw him in the post office and told him I was not going to issue him another license. I told him I would issue him a permit for a week or so, and if they still wanted to get married after that, to come see me for the license. He laughed and now reminds me often of what I told him.

Many of the people I married were going through our county to, or returning from, Panama City Beach. Florida does not require a waiting period anymore for out-of-state individuals to purchase a marriage license. Many couples decided to just go ahead and tie the knot on the way to "the world's most beautiful beaches," as the advertisements claim.

There were ceremonies I performed in which I had some reservation concerning the citizenship status of the man. The law in Florida allows an illegal person to get married as long as we suggest they do the paperwork to become legal. Many times the individual could not understand what was being said without an interpreter. He would simply nod when they told him to, and we would make it through the ceremony.

I married couples who looked like they were sincere and some who were nonchalant about it. If the couple did not act serious I devised a ceremony that I called the short version, which basically said, "Do you take this woman to be your wife, and do you take this man to be your husband?"

Unlike surrounding states there is no waiting period in Florida between getting a divorce and applying for a new marriage license. It was not uncommon for someone to get a divorce upstairs with the circuit judge, then come right down to the clerk's office and get a license to marry a different person.

BURYING

I guess this is as good a time as any to tell you about Taylor's Corollary. After watching families fight over what Mom and Dad left, I came to this opinion: Many times the love and concern that people show for their parents is directly proportional to the money, land, and other assets they have. It is a sad commentary for parents to work all their lives just to have their children fight over what is left.

Estate planning can solve many family arguments. Someone told me a story that pretty well sums up this situation. A grandfather was in the hospital, and his grandchildren were visiting. The visit was about to be over when one of the little boys got up on the bed next to his grandfather and asked him if he would sound like a frog. The startled grandfather asked the boy, "Why in the world do you want me to sound like a frog?" The little boy answered, "Mom says when you croak we're all going to Disney World."

One of the saddest situations I had to deal with was an individual dying and no one claiming the body. The law in Florida requires counties to pay for the burial of indigent people who have no kin to claim the body. The law also allows the county to decide the type of burial. Years ago Holmes County decided if the county was responsible for payment, they would select the most economical way, cremation. Before the county can cremate an unclaimed body, the medical examiner's office must offer the body to Shands Teaching Hospital, located at the University of Florida in Gainesville.

In Florida any unattended death has to be sent to the medical examiner's office unless a doctor will sign the death certificate. This requirement causes hardship for the family dealing with the death of a loved one. Often the family has difficulty in planning the funeral because the medical examiner's office for our circuit is in Panama City. The medical examiner can do a short version of an autopsy or a full autopsy. The counties of the Fourteenth Judicial Circuit, rather than the state of Florida, shared the cost of the medical examiner's office. This is one of the state mandates that the state never funded but should have years ago.

One thing I have noticed is when someone dies; most people try to find something good to say about him or her, even if they have to look hard to find it. Jack Faircloth tells the story of the death of a man in the community who was a real outlaw. Everybody wondered how the preacher was going to handle his funeral. They found out quickly when the preacher's opening prayer said, "Dear Lord, bless the family of the recently departed, and may he go to where we know he ain't."

* * *

CHAPTER 7

COUNSELOR AND ADVOCATE

It was amazing to me the number of people who came to the clerk's office for advice. People would seek my advice on everything from raising children to settling landline disputes. One day a local man came by to see me about his child support. Much to his dismay, he was paying child support on several children. He had never been married to any of the women he had children with. In desperation, some of the women had obtained public assistance for the children. Since the law in Florida requires the father to repay the state for any public assistance paid, the state had garnished the fellow's paycheck. He worked for a local farmer and only made a little over three hundred dollars a week. He came and asked me what he should do. I had known him for years, and I jokingly told him that I would learn Spanish and move to Spain because they would not extradite him back for child support. We both laughed, and after finishing our conversation he left. Several weeks later the guy took one of his kids and went to Washington State and did not tell the mother where he was. That of course is against the federal law, so the FBI soon had him rounded up and brought him and the child back to Florida. The feds realized that he was not really a threat and were lenient on him. I always wondered if he was on his way to Spain when they caught him.

Many times I have found that people want someone to give them advice but very few ever actually take the advice. Through the years many couples came to talk to me about getting a divorce. I always advised them to try to work things out if possible. I would then tell them if reconciliation was not possible, be cordial. It is sad to say that I could probably count on one hand the number of cordial divorces that I have ever seen. The judge always had to settle all the issues, including who got the kids on what weekend and who had primary custody. It seems that more times than not both sides were unhappy with the settlement.

Elected officials have to know the difference between advice and legal advice. When I first became clerk it was standard procedure for the clerk to prepare deeds and other documents. It did not take me long to realize that this should be done by an attorney.

Every political cycle people came by to ask for political advice about whether or not to run for this office or that office. I have a standard answer for those wanting to run for sheriff: I ask them how they like the dairy business. They always look at me like I am crazy, and say they would not like the dairy business. I then tell them that the sheriff's job is twenty-four-seven, just like the dairy business, so consider that.

For other offices I tell them that I did not stay in office all these years by getting involved in other people's races. I also tell them that it has been my experience that someone asking you about running for office is like someone asking your advice about getting married. When someone has made up their mind to do either, you cannot talk them out of it. They just have to try it and see how it works. It has always been my policy to not even let the deputy clerks in my office know how I intended to vote, and unlike what many folks think I have never told any of them how they should cast their vote. There seems to be a belief among some people that all the elected officials in the courthouse get together every election and decide who they should support for every office. Since the tax collector and property appraiser are no longer in the courthouse and the sheriff was never in the courthouse, most of the rumors about elected officials conspiring in politics went by the wayside.

A friend of mine in Bonifay came to see to if I could help two policemen get into the state game warden program. Neither had heard anything from the applications they had submitted. The class for the new recruits was to start the next week. I told him I would see what I could do. I called Senator Pat Thomas, who for all the years I had known him was always ready to help any way he could. After I explained to Senator Thomas what I wanted, he said, "Cody, you may be in luck, the head of the Game and Freshwater Fish Commission is in my outer office right now." I gave him the two names, and he told me he would call me back. The senator called back and told me that he had good news. He said the two policemen from Bonifay were not in the final group but were on the waiting lists. Several who had been selected had decided not to take their slots, so the director agreed to give both of the Bonifay policemen a slot for the next class. They were told to be in Tallahassee on Monday to start the class. He said that someone from the department would call them with all the details. One of the policemen went and has served the department well; the other policeman declined to go and later became a Holmes County deputy sheriff. I learned from this that you may not always get instant results for someone you want to help.

One of my most interesting stories of helping someone involved a man named Tony Scavetta. As the locals tell the story, Tony was on a Greyhound bus headed to Marianna, Florida to visit some relatives. He spoke very little English, and somehow he ended up in Bonifay. A local realtor sold Tony a house before he realized he was not in Marianna. Someone told him to see me and I would help him with his citizenship forms. Tony came to the clerk's office, and sure enough, we completed his application for citizenship after several hours at the typewriter. He tried to pay me, but I refused. I told him that was part of my job and he did not owe me anything. He informed me that a Scavetta paid his debts and insisted I go by his house that afternoon for him to give me something. My three boys were all young and had come to the courthouse after school, so I took them with me to Tony's house.

We walked in and sat down at a table set with five wine glasses poured full of homemade wine Tony had made. I was a teetotaling Baptist deacon sitting there not knowing what to do. Thankfully the Lord provided a way out. Luke, my youngest son, said right out that he needed to go to the restroom. Tony jumped up and said he would show Luke to the way. While they were gone, I poured all the wine down the kitchen drain. Tony returned and saw the empty glasses and said, "Oh, you liked the wine," and poured us another round. I told him I appreciated it but one glass was enough. He then proceeded to his garden, where he picked some nice vegetables to send home with me. As we were getting into the truck Tony went back in the house and brought out a half gallon of his homemade wine for me to take home to my wife. I thanked him and took the vegetables and the wine and went home. When I got home and told Brenda the story, she laughed as she prepared the vegetables for supper and poured the wine down the sink.

One afternoon at my home I had a group of deacons from a local church came to see me. They knew I was a deacon in my church, and they wanted my advice on a problem they had. The problem was concerning their pastor. The church had voted to fire him, but he would not leave. They wanted to know how we, the deacons at our church, would handle a situation like this. The question caught me off guard, and I did not know what to say. I think the Lord may have given me some divine wisdom, as it came to me to tell them to have the chief of police be there the next Sunday. They thanked me and went on their way. The chief of police was there the next Sunday and told the preacher that he could not come on the church grounds. The preacher got in his car and left, and that ended the problem, at least for a while.

A few weeks went by, and the deacons came back to see me again. The problem this time was the new preacher the church had hired. He was a young pastor from Alabama, and someone had told the deacons he was frequenting the dog track in Ebro, Florida. All the deacons went to the dog track one night, and one bought a ticket to go inside. Shortly, he saw the pastor watching the races. The pastor saw the deacon and said, "Deacon, what are you doing here?" The deacon replied, "Pastor, what are *you* doing here?" The deacon went back and reported to the church what he had witnessed. The church voted to fire the pastor, but he refused to leave, so they were back at square one. I told them the police chief was still a good option. They thanked me and went to talk to the chief. The chief was again at the church the next Sunday and told the preacher to hit the road, and he finally agreed to go. The next pastor the church called turned out to be a good one. Thank goodness my services were no longer needed.

There was another time that I was able to help someone by being in the right place at the right time. Lonnie Hagans had been a deputy sheriff in Holmes County for several years. Some of his political enemies found an old misdemeanor charge from when he was a young man. He'd pled to a minor charge and paid a fine. His civil rights were not taken away, so he had no problem getting his certification to serve as a deputy. Because someone filed a complaint with state police standards, an investigation was conducted. Lonnie's lawyer was able to have the hearing to determine his status held in Bonifay. The state offered an agreement: the state would not take his certification, and in return, he would resign from the sheriff's department and agree not to work in law enforcement anymore. Lonnie was within six months of retirement. He contacted Marlin Register and I about helping him get a state job for six months to finish out his retirement.

At this point we turned to Richard Kelly who was the assistant commissioner of agriculture under Doyle Conner. Marlin and I both knew Richard, since we both had served as FFA state officers and he was the state advisor during our service. We called Richard and asked him if he could give Lonnie a job for the six months to complete his retirement. He told us told he would. Lonnie went to work, but about a week later, Richard called me to say that someone had called him and told him that he had just hired a mighty rough character. I told Richard to calm down, that many good people in Holmes County were rough, and just give him a little time. He agreed to the trial period. Lonnie was a very capable worker, performing his duties well. He worked several months past the six and was able to retire with full retirement benefits.

In another instance, I walked into the court department one day, met a young man, and asked if I could help him. He said one of my deputies had told him what he needed. For some reason, however, he caused me to think that he might have something else on his mind. I asked him if there was something I could do for him. He told me that he had just gotten out of prison and that he thought he had found a job, but he owed the clerks twenty dollars on an old traffic fine. He went on to say he did not have the money. For some reason I took a twenty-dollar bill out of my pocket. I told him that I was going to make an investment in him and to go pay the fine and get his license. He thanked me and went on his way. I did not what his name was until one of the deputy clerks told me.

Several months later, his father called me and told me that he wanted to thank me for helping his son. He asked me if I knew that his son had been killed in a car accident a while back. I told him I did not know about the accident. He said that when his son went to get his license, he had agreed to be an organ donor. At the last count, nine people had been helped by his donations. Doctors had told the family that his organs had saved several lives. The man broke down as he told me what had happened, and as I listened to his story, so did I. It reminded me again that God expects us to reach out and help people when given the opportunity. Doing so could impact the lives of many others we know nothing about.

* * *

CHAPTER 8

STATE LEADERS

Since Holmes County did not have a county manager I was able in my role as clerk to work with state leaders to obtain funding for many projects. I will list here some of projects and legislation that I worked on with those leaders.

Senator Pat Thomas and Senator Dempsey Barron represented Holmes County in the Florida Senate when I first took office. Senator Thomas was much more approachable than Senator Barron. Senator Thomas tried to return every phone call and be of service to all citizens. He had a great office staff headed by his long-time secretary, Betty Edwards.

There is an interesting story of how Senator Thomas acquired a state prison for Bonifay. State Representative Big Sam Mitchell approached the Holmes County Board of County Commissioners and asked if the county wanted a state prison. The commission took the political way out and held a public hearing on the matter, causing a big crowd to show up. The crowd was equally divided on the issue, so the board took no action. Representative Mitchell decided he was through trying to get a prison for Holmes County. Instead he would try to get one for his home county of Washington. The site he chose was on the University of Florida beef unit just east of Chipley. He got a great deal of opposition.

Meanwhile back in Holmes County, Cecil Motley had taken over as the chamber director. He took a different approach to obtaining a correctional facility for the county by canvasing the community, talking with the people. He asked them if they would support something that would bring over four hundred jobs to the county. The majority of the citizens agreed with him. A group then approached Senator Thomas about the possibility of getting a state prison for the county. Representative Mitchell was still trying to get the prison for Washington County, and he let it be known he would not support a prison for Holmes County until Washington County got theirs.

I was in contact with Senator Thomas concerning the prison for Holmes County during the legislative session. He reported that it did not look good. Senator Barron wanted a prison for Calhoun County, and that site was ahead of Holmes County. When the session was drawing to a close, a senator from South Florida decided he did not want a prison in his district. Senator Barron told Senator Thomas that he would help him get it for Holmes County. Senator Thomas called me at home late in the legislative session and told me what had happened. He asked me if I was sure that people here really wanted the prison, and I told him I was sure. He told me he was going to announce the prison for Holmes County in a press release in the morning without telling Representative Mitchell. The next morning he released the information and later told me that Representative Mitchell was really upset with him.

Tommy Speights, the public information officer for the Florida Department of Transportation, told me that Representative Mitchell had guaranteed him that he would get the prison for Washington County on the beef unit site before Holmes County got a prison. He said Big Sam had told him that if he didn't get the prison on the beef unit site he would "kiss his butt on the front steps of the state capitol and give him two weeks to draw a crowd." Tommy said he had to remind Big Sam about not getting the prison, and Big Sam just laughed it off. A couple of years later he did get a prison for Washington but not on the beef unit site and not before Holmes County got one. Senator Thomas always said it was Senator Barron who had gotten the prison for the county, not him. I think the truth of the matter is if it had not been for his relationship with Senator Barron, we would not have gotten it. You can find very few folks in the county who oppose the prison today. It provides jobs for the county's citizens and also purchases many goods and services from local businesses. A work camp has been added to the prison, and that opened more job opportunities for Holmes County and the surrounding counties.

Senator Barron had been a Democrat for years in the Florida Senate, but in later years changed to the Republican Party and made efforts to get others to change parties also. One day I got a call from Judge Robert Earl Brown, who told me that Senator Barron wanted to invite all the elected officials from Holmes County to his ranch, south of Bonifay, for a steak dinner on a certain night the next week. We met at the courthouse and rode to his ranch in my van. As we headed to the Barron ranch someone asked what this was all about. The judge informed us that there was going to be a Tallahassee VIP there to try to persuade us to change to the Republican Party.

When we arrived at the ranch, the senator's girlfriend (and later wife), Terri Jo, greeted us. Secretary of State Jim Smith was the surprise visitor from Tallahassee. We had some general conversation, and then we were served our dinner, beef stew. I never have been too fond of beef stew, so the meal did not impress me. After dinner they gave us the next surprise. We were informed that Governor Martinez was going to call in and wanted to talk to us. The governor called, and apparently he had been told that we were ready to change parties. He wanted to set a date for us to come to Tallahassee to make our party changeover public. It caught all of us off guard. Just when it looked like no one was going to speak, Judge Brown spoke up. He said, "Governor, we are all still thinking about the change and we will let you know what we decide." The governor thanked us and said his good-byes.

As we headed back to Bonifay we discussed the party change. Apparently their appeal was not too successful and none of the officials changed at that time.

I have not always been proud of the Democrat Party, but neither am I proud of the Republicans. Sometimes I think I will do what the father of our great nation, George Washington, did about party membership. Most people do not realize that George Washington was not a member of a political party. He warned in his farewell address that the allegiance to party over nation was a detriment to the well-being of the country, and today we see he was correct.

When I took office in January of 1977 the county was just getting over the removal of three of its county commissioners. Governor Askew had removed the commissioners based on a grand jury report that had accused them of misfeasance in office. The Florida Senate reinstated two of the suspended commissioners. The other commissioner was actually convicted of a misdemeanor for damaging some county road equipment. The county had to pay the two reinstated commissioners their back pay for the time they were removed until the end of their terms. The money amounted to a little over $25,000. The order to pay them came after I became clerk, and the county had to pay the money.

It bothered me that the state did not pay the money since the governor of the state had removed them and the Florida Senate overturned his removal. I asked Senator Thomas if he would try to have the money returned to the county. He told me he would try. That year he placed the money in the budget, but Governor Askew vetoed it, saying in his message that the state repaying the county was not a legal expenditure. The next couple of years Senator Thomas put the money in the state budget again only to be vetoed by Askew. Governor Bob Graham replaced Askew, and the first year of his term, Senator Thomas put in our request to get the $25,000 back for the county. Governor Graham vetoed the request the first couple of times that the senator put it in. One day Senator Thomas called me with good news. He was the chairman of the Senate Appropriations Committee, and the governor had called him and wanted him to add several highway patrolmen for Dade County and some other items. The senator told him he would be happy to give him the patrolmen but there were some things that he wanted. One of the things he wanted was the $25,000 for Holmes County. What had been illegal for six vetoes now was legal in the political tradeoff that Senator Thomas made with the governor. Governor Graham did not veto the money, and we were so proud that we were finally going to be repaid for the money the former commissioners had received.

Around the same time, the Holmes County sheriff had gotten in a budget dispute with the board of commissioners and had appealed his budget to the governor and cabinet. The state budget was completed with the $25,000 in it, and shortly afterward

Sheriff Galloway's appeal hit Tallahassee. The commission and I had to go to Tallahassee to testify before the administrative commission. They would then make the final recommendation to the governor as to how much money the sheriff got, if any. The board and I were trying our best to poor-mouth, and then one of members of the commission asked about the $25,000. They already knew about it, and after we finished testifying the commission recommended that the sheriff get the $25,000. The governor and cabinet agreed, and the sheriff got our money. After it was said and done I was sorry I had ever asked for the money.

RECREATIONAL CENTER

Ironically, the county got involved in one of the biggest controversies on record by mistake. In 1986 the local newspaper editor and the sheriff asked Senator Pat Thomas for money to build a recreation center in the city of Bonifay. The county commission did not request the money and was in no way involved with the project. The project that was envisioned by the editor and the sheriff included some baseball fields and a firing range for the sheriff's department. Senator Thomas agreed to put in the "turkey" request which is a state appropriation for a local project, and it was funded. The problem was instead of the money going to the city of Bonifay it was placed in the name of the Holmes County Board of County Commissioners. The first time the board knew that they were getting the money was when the newspaper announced the project had been funded. The board checked with the state agency to see if the city could handle the project instead of the county. The agency said yes, but the county would still be responsible for the administration of funds. So the county was put in a position of administering a grant that it did not ask for.

The board did appoint a citizens committee to make recommendations for what should be included in the facility. The committee came up with several ball fields, a gym, a pool, and a lighted walking track. Later, handball courts were included. Many citizens were opposed to the project and were very vocal from the beginning. One of the county commissioners who was on the board at the time often said that the first shovel of dirt that was turned for the recreational center was also the first shovel that dug his political grave.

Thankfully, the board was careful to bid everything in the project, even down to the equipment for the gym. Someone got so upset with the idea of the recreation center that they filed complaints with the Florida Department of Law Enforcement. The project progressed, and the final grant amounts received totaled one million dollars. The investigation that FDLE conducted was really very good for the county in the long run. Several agents came by and looked at the records, and after seeing that the county had bid all the work and had kept good records, they concluded that there was no wrongdoing on the part of the county. This made some people even madder. It even prompted some of them to want to defeat any elected official who had been in any way connected with the project, including me.

Consequently, a local feed store operator was talked into trying to unseat me. He started a mean campaign of personal smears. Thank goodness the citizens of the county looked beyond his bull, and I beat him in every precinct in the county. I went with the theory to make a positive out of the recreation center. The county had a big grand opening for the center right in the middle of the campaign and had all the news media present. When people saw what had been constructed and realized that their children and grandchildren were playing on some of the best fields around, the public perception of the project began to improve. By election time my opponent was singing in the wind with no one listening. It reminded me of one of my old basketball sayings: "The best defense is a good offense."

Other projects that Senator Thomas helped Holmes County to obtain were the state prison, the agriculture building, the first phase of the new fairgrounds, the money to build and furnish the new county health department, and several road improvements projects. I am sure I left out some things, but Senator Pat Thomas served Holmes County well. He died several years ago, and Holmes County lost a dear friend.

In 1992, after reapportionment, W. D. Childers became our senator, and what a change he was from Senator Thomas. His nickname was the "Banty Rooster," and it did not take long to find out why when you dealt with him. Johnny Manuel was a member of the local Bonifay Businessmen's Club, which leased a campsite from one of the paper companies that owned property along the Choctawhatchee River. The Northwest Florida Water Management District bought the land and gave all the leaseholders two years to get off the property. Johnny came to see me and told me that he heard that W. D. Childers was going to speak at the Bonifay Kiwanis club luncheon the next Wednesday. He wondered if I would talk to the senator with him about getting the lease on their camp renewed or, if there was a possibility, allowing the club to trade the state four acres they owned in the area. W. D. spoke at the meeting that day, and it was a colorful speech, laced with what some folks considered profanity. He mentioned before he got through that every word he had used was in the Bible and, therefore, he did not consider it profanity.

After the meeting Johnny and I went up and talked to him about the hunting club's situation. By the way, I should offer this disclaimer: I am not now nor have I ever been a member of the Bonifay

Businessmen's Club. The senator listened to what we had to say; I thought that he would say something like "Let me get with the department and I'll get back with you all." But W. D. told Johnny and me that he would take care of the problem.

A couple of weeks went by, and I got a call from Roger Robinson, a Childers aide, who told me that Senator Childers wanted to talk to me. He informed me that he had the problem with the camp taken care of. He was the chairman of the committee that approved the water management's budget. When he got to Tallahassee after talking to us, he removed three top positions from their budget. The water management director came to see the senator and wanted to talk to him. He told him that he was not available to talk to him because he had some friends in Holmes County who were worried about their lease. The senator told him when the problem with the lease was settled, he would be glad to talk to him. Senator Childers sent word to the director that he wanted the department to swap the two acres they owned for the four that the club owned. The director countered with an offer to deed the two acres to the county and let the county lease the property to the club. He called me to inform me of the solution and to see if the county would agree to be part of the agreement. I told him I would discuss it with the board and get back to him.

Fortunately, the board agreed to be the conduit for the club. The club got their clubhouse, and the county residents got a nice boat ramp. The water management district got four acres, and their top three positions were put back in the budget, and everybody was happy. Several years later W. D. was term-limited out of the legislature and was elected as a county commissioner in Escambia County.

Senator Durelle Peaden was elected as our state senator after W. D. Childers was term-limited out. Senator Peaden had been our state representative and was well liked in Holmes County. I had a closer relationship with him than with any of our legislators since Senator Pat Thomas. He obtained most of the funding for the Holmes County Fairgrounds with help from State Representative Don Brown. Senator Peaden also helped get courthouse funding to correct the ADA deficiencies.

HOSPITAL CORPORATION

The Florida legislature established the Holmes County Hospital Corporation in the early 1950s for the sole purpose of building and operating a hospital in Holmes County. It was created in a way to keep local politics out of the process. The governor appoints the members of the hospital board, and so the county commissioners have no control over the board. The process has served the county well, and since it is not a county hospital, the county has no liability for its operation or debts. The original hospital was built as a Hill-Burton Hospital in 1955 and was financed with some of the county's racetrack funds. When the hospital was paid off, the Florida legislature changed the racetrack formula so that the funds that had previously been going to the hospital now went toward construction of a new county health department.

The hospital board decided to build a new hospital. They bought property on the southeast quadrant of I-10 and started plans to finance and build the new facility. It came to light that there was a debt service limit of $250,000 in their original charter and they could not borrow more than the original limit. With the construction of the new facility estimated at seventeen million dollars, they had hit a snag. The chairperson of the hospital board called me in the spring of 2005. She asked me if I could talk to Senator Peaden about sponsoring legislation to remove the debt limit that was holding up plans for the new hospital. I told her that I would be glad to call Senator Peaden, who was also a medical doctor.

Senator Peaden told me that it was too late in the legislative process to introduce local legislative changes unless the senate legal staff could find a way. The senate lawyer reported back to Senator Peaden that there was a way that he could get something introduced if no other senator objected. Senator Peaden agreed to put in the legislation, and thankfully no one objected. He added one stipulation, since the original authorization was approved by local county referendum, he would have the same requirement on the new authorization.

The hospital board enlisted the help of Dr. Beverly Helms and others to help with the referendum to raise the debt limit. The group put on a good public relations campaign in support of raising the debt limit and it was overwhelming approved. The hospital has since been constructed.

NATIONAL GUARD

Another community project that I was involved in concerned the projected closing of local Florida National Guard unit. I had served in the guard for six years in the Panama City unit and knew many of the soldiers in the Bonifay unit. As a medic I was assigned to the unit during training exercises and summer camp. Roy Messer, a sergeant in the local unit, came to see me one day and told me that the local unit had received word that it was about to be integrated into the Chipley or Defuniak Springs Unit. He wanted to know if I would go to Tallahassee with him to talk with the governor about leaving the unit open. I told him I would be glad to go, then went by the First Bank of Holmes County and enlisted the aid of Shouppe Howell, the president of the bank.

Mr. Howell knew Lieutenant Governor Wayne Mixon well and called him to get us an appointment with the governor, who at the time was Bob Graham. We got the appointment and Mr. Howell, Roy Messer, and I went to Tallahassee to see the governor.

When we arrived the governor had been called out of town on an emergency, and the lieutenant governor met with us on the governor's behalf. We apprised Mr. Mixon of the problem, and he seemed surprised that he had not been aware of the reorganization. He told us that the governor had promised him that he would be in on any decision affecting Northwest Florida and he would talk to the governor about the situation. He also set up a meeting with the adjutant general of the State National Guard to come to Bonifay for a public meeting to explain his reorganization.

The general came to Bonifay on a Sunday morning. Apparently he thought everyone would be in church. He was wrong; the locals do usually go to church on Sunday, but on that Sunday morning, they went to see the general. The armory was full of people, and when Mr. Howell and I, along with many others, got up to speak, the general began to see the light. A couple of weeks later the governor announced that the Bonifay National Guard Unit would remain intact.

The unit is still in Bonifay some thirty years later and was activated with some unit soldiers being deployed to Iraq and Afghanistan. Thank the good Lord all made it home safely; the country is most appreciative of their service.

Small County Aid

Several years ago, Representative Don Brown put forth the idea of giving small counties more state money. He put in the request at the urging of several small county leaders, including me and clerks from Liberty and Lafayette Counties, Robert Hill and Rickey Lyons. The first year his idea got nowhere. The next year, with backing from and the hard work of Chris Doolin and the small county coalition, the bill was passed. It gave small counties some fiscally constrained money that has been their salvation. This small group was able to convince then governor Jeb Bush of the need, and finally the legislature agreed to help. Small counties will always be indebted to Don Brown for helping get the additional funding from the Florida legislature.

Governor Bob Graham

As I was writing some material for this book and looking over some of my old papers, I got a call from Robert Nabors, who served as general counsel to Governor Bob Graham. It was so ironic that Bob called me out of the blue and told me that through the years he had kept a letter that I had written to Governor Graham concerning help for small counties. He said he wanted to send the letter to me because it had had a profound influence on the governor taking the initiative to do some things that have helped small counties. I include my letter and the letter that Bob Nabors sent me in the appendix. (See appendix B, B2, B3, B4.) The economic viability of counties in Florida is largely determined by one thing—access to the Gulf of Mexico or the Atlantic Ocean. The financial help that the Florida legislature has provided small counties has allowed them to stay solvent.

Senator Jim Scott

I have dealt with other legislators who have been very helpful to Holmes County too. Former senator Jim Scott of Broward County actually bought a farm in Holmes County years ago and became our part-time resident senator. The late Senator Pat Thomas introduced me to him and his business partner Norman Tripp. Norman owned a ranch next to Senator Scott's in Holmes County. Senator Barron, Pat Thomas, Jim Scott, and W. D. Childers would sometimes congregate at Senator Scott's ranch when they had a break in the legislative session. They would invite me, Herman Laramore, the public defender for the circuit, and other folks to just have a down-home cookout and talk politics. I mostly listened to these gentlemen, who at the time were the leaders of the Florida Senate and the most powerful men in Tallahassee. The news media would have given anything to have listened to some of the discussions that we were privy to.

After Senator Scott, who was a Republican, was term-limited out of office, he was the legal counsel to the Senate on reapportionment committee for the 2000 census. I found out that a proposed congressional map split Holmes County into two congressional districts. The supervisor of elections at the time, Debbie Morris, called and told me about the county being split and what a nightmare it was for her to split precincts. She asked me if I could call someone in an effort to get it changed. I called Senator Scott and told him the situation; he told me he would check on our problem. The next week a *new* proposed map came out with Holmes County in one district entirely.

In February of 2011 I ran into Jim Scott in Tallahassee at the clerk's legislative days. We had a nice conversation, and he told me how Debbie Morris's phone call to me and my call to him may have changed history. He said that a senator told him one day that when he made the change that put Holmes County in one congressional district, it also moved a state Senate line that he lived in and kept him from running for the state Senate that year. He went on to say that the senator was not too upset with him, since he got elected later and became the Senate president. I cannot say for sure the change was made because of our request, but it happened.

I call these legislators the old guard of the Florida legislature, and today they are all gone. Most have been replaced because of term limits that have not served the best interests of the citizens of Florida. The problem I have seen with term limits is that they have made the legislative staff and the bureaucrats in Tallahassee too powerful. If we are going to have term limits on legislators, there should be the same limits on the legislative staff. The way I see it, we have always had term limits; they are called elections. If citizens do not like who is representing them, they have the right to change that on Election Day.

* * *

CHAPTER 9

Courthouse Humor

I must provide a little disclaimer to the humorous stories I am about to disclose. I cannot say that I personally witnessed all the stories that I write about. Thirty-six years of court cases make it difficult to remember exactly which stories I personally observed and which ones were part of court proceedings and related stories.

The first story I attribute to former assistant state attorney Joe Sheffield, who told of having a trial going on in Jackson County, Florida. There had been a fight in a bar and a lady had been cut. The lady was on the stand and was testifying as to what happened. The state attorney asked her if she had been in the bar that night and she said she had. He asked if she saw a fight break out, and she said she did. He asked her if she had been cut in the fracas. She thought just a minute and stood up, made a motion across her lower abdomen, and said, "No, I did not get cut in the fracas; I got cut about six inches above." Young attorneys sometimes find out the hard way that you must be careful how you pose a question to a witness.

We had a trial going one day, and the state had done a good job of establishing the fact that the defendant had shot the victim. When the defense attorney got his shot at the state's star witness, he began to question the fact that the eye witness had identified his client from a long distance away. The defense attorney was not making any headway with the witness's credibility, so he finally asked the witness in a frustrated tone, "Sir, just how far can you see?" The witness, an elderly gentleman, paused and very humbly answered, "Well, son, how far is the moon?" The defense attorney, realizing he had asked one question too many, just sat down.

An answer to a question in one memorable case created quite a stir when the entire courtroom erupted into laughter at the response. The attorney was questioning the witness, an elderly man, as he attempted to provide background information to the jury.
After going through an elaborate questioning to establish who was married to whom, and for how long, the attorney said to the man, "So you have been married to the same woman for fifty years, is that correct?" The old man thought a moment and said emphatically, "No, mister, she ain't the same."

Another story I heard about long marriages is very amusing. A man and his wife had been married for fifty years. The children wanted to have a fiftieth wedding anniversary celebration, and the parents agreed. The big party went well until the afternoon; after everyone had left, the wife noticed the man over in the corner acting like he was sad. She went over to him and said, "What in world are you thinking? We just had a great time, and you are acting all depressed and sad." He responded by saying, "Do you remember the night fifty years ago that your dad caught us kissing on the swing on the front porch?" She said, "Yes, I do." The man continued, "He told me that if I didn't marry you, he was going to have me put in jail for fifty years. I was just sitting here thinking…tonight, I would have been a free man."

The courthouse janitors have always been a humorous crew. Most were hired more for their political pull than their ability to clean. When I first was elected there were three janitors. Jesse Richardson was the only black man of the crew, and he was very active in city and county politics. The school board at the time occupied offices in the basement, and Jack Davis and Robert Hall were two of the staff members. Robert was the mayor of Bonifay, and one day as Jesse was picking up the trash Jack asked him if the folks in his neighborhood were going to support Robert in his reelection bid. Robert was not in that day, so Jesse felt free to talk to Jack. He told him they were not going to support Mr. Robert in the election. He went on to say that they were going to do like a little bunny and hop right over Mr. Robert's name and vote for the other person. Jesse did not realize, however, that Jack was recording what he said. The next day when he came by for the garbage and the mayor was in, Jack told Jesse he wanted him to hear something. He turned on the recorder and it played their conversation from the day before. Jesse broke out in a sweat and finally told the mayor that he was only kidding and that he was going to support him. They all had a good laugh, and Robert was reelected.

One day one of the deputy clerks in the court department called me to come back to the court department and deal with an irate customer. A local fellow who was a World War II veteran was being unruly. It seemed his daughter had signed a Baker Act petition on him, and he had been released. He was mad with Judge Brown, the judge who had signed the order committing him. He was also mad with me since my name was on the forms and with Sheriff Dennis Lee because one of his deputies had taken him to Panama City for evaluation. He had come to the clerk's office to see who had signed the papers committing him. When I showed him it was his daughter, he became even more irate. He started cursing and talking bad about Judge Brown and his neighbor, who had recently died. He announced in front of all the ladies that he was going to the city cemetery and take a whiz on the man's grave. I told him to stop the cursing, but he just stepped it up a notch. I told one of the deputy clerks to call the sheriff's department, and he left.

A few days later I was in Bowen Hardware, over behind some high shelves. The fellow came in and hollered to Bill Parrish, one of the owners, and asked him if he had a fish fryer. He said, "I am going to have a fish fry for all my friends, but I tell you who won't be there." He started naming names, starting with Judge Brown, Sheriff Lee, and me. He could not see me from where he was, and all the workers knew of the problem that he and I had had recently. Finally I stepped out from behind the shelves and called the guy's name and said, "Why don't you go ahead and tell the rest of the story?" The man froze for a minute and, gaining his composure, said, "Cody kicked me out for cussing." I said, "Tell them the rest." He then told them about the cemetery threat and turned around and walked out. He just never could come to grips with the fact that his daughter had signed the papers to have him evaluated; it was just a lot easier to blame someone else.

Clyde Brown was the most revered and respected attorney I ever knew. He was in practice when I was elected. He was also a great storyteller. Periodically he would stop by my office and tell me some of the most interesting and humorous stories about the history of Holmes County. One of his most famous statements concerning the Florida legislature seemed to always be true; he said, "Your life, liberty, and property are never safe as long as the Florida legislature is in session." It is amazing how Mr. Brown's wisdom has stood the test of time.

During one of Mr. Brown's visits to my office he told me how the new county courthouse was built. He said A. P. Drummond, another local attorney, called him one day and told him that he had a grand jury in session. Mr. Drummond was the county prosecuting attorney and worked with the local grand jury. He asked Clyde to draft a true bill for the grand jury stating that the county records were not safe-housed in the existing courthouse. He drafted the presentment for the grand jury and returned it to Mr. Drummond. As predicted, the grand jury returned the presentment that recommended a new courthouse be built. The two of them decided it would be better if they came out against the new courthouse. They figured that declaration on their part would increase the chances that the citizens would be in favor of the idea. He said there were just some folks in the county who were going to be against anything he and Mr. Drummond were for. When the word got out that the two of them opposed the new courthouse, the county commissioners and the citizens could not wait to get started. In 1965 the new courthouse was completed.

The funniest story that Clyde told me was about a Holmes County sheriff who was a client of his. He said the sheriff came by his office and wanted to know if he could go with him to Tallahassee the next day to see the governor. The governor had wanted to see the sheriff about some complaints he had received from citizens of the county. So the next day Clyde and the sheriff went to see the governor. After exchanging introductions, the governor opened a folder. He told the sheriff that he was holding in his hand the executive order that would remove him from office for allowing bootlegging and houses of ill repute to operate wide open in Holmes County. Clyde said since he was the lawyer he was sitting there trying to think of what to say.

The sheriff, however, was not at a loss for words as he quickly responded to the governor's comments. He told the governor that he might want to stop and ponder that a little bit before he signed that order. He asked the governor if he remembered how close his election had been, and the governor nodded his agreement. The sheriff asked him if he remembered that on two different occasions that election night, someone on his staff had called to Holmes County to see if they had come up with additional votes. He reminded the governor that on both occasions he rounded up the votes that they had requested. The sheriff went on to say that if he signed that order he was going back by the Tallahassee Democrat and hand them the proof of the illegal votes.

Clyde said it was deadly silent for what seemed like an eternity, and then the governor broke the silence by saying, "Well, Sheriff, could you at least hold it down a little?" Clyde said, "I was flabbergasted. I went as the sheriff's lawyer and did not say a word."

There are many stories of voting irregularities and their effects on elections before voting machines were instituted. Voting machines did more to clean up the voting process and increase the likelihood of accurate election results than anything that had previously been tried. Marlin Register was the supervisor of elections when the first machines were put into use. He said that he had a terrible time convincing some of the men of the county to let their wives go into the voting booth and vote by themselves. The law only allowed help for a voter if they couldn't read or were disabled. Marlin said one man told him that he slept with his wife and he was blame sure going to vote with her too. It took a while, but Marlin made the voters follow the law. He also said that many of the women would tell him privately that they appreciated being able to vote without interference from their husbands.

Clyde told me of another Holmes County elections story. He said the county judge's race was so close that the absentees would likely decide the race. The election was held using paper ballots, so the canvassing board decided to wait until the next day to count the absentees since it was so late at night. During this period of time Florida law stated that if anyone could prove that any of the absentee ballots had been tampered with, then all of them would be thrown out. The final results without the absentees would stand. The next morning when people began driving into Bonifay they noticed pieces of paper strewn up and down Waukesha Street. Upon further examination it was discovered that the pieces of paper were the uncounted absentee ballots. He said they never found out who had tampered with the ballots, but the judge candidate who was ahead in the count the night before was declared the winning candidate when the absentees were thrown out.

The day Clyde died; I wrote a poem in his honor, which I gave to his family. His son-in-law, Jackson Beatty, an outstanding attorney in his own right, called one day and asked me if he could have my permission to include my poem into a family album in memory of Mr. Brown, and I, of course, agreed. I include this poem not because I believe it to be a great literary work, but because it accurately conveys my feelings for a great gentleman and a fine county lawyer.

CLYDE BROWN

A lawyer by trade, a gentleman by birth;
He touched so many lives upon this earth.
He never acted proud or haughty, as lesser men might do,
But made you proud to call him friend and I do.
He was kind and generous, an example for us all,
A man among men—he stood tall.

He finished his work, closed his case,
He had his last hearing, he ran his last race.

I can only believe as complex as this world has become,
The Lord needed a lawyer to advise Him some.
He did what so many have done before,
He decided to knock on Clyde Brown's door.
The Lord said, "Clyde, I accept your final appeal,
Enter My son and in my court, kneel."
As a lawyer you have enjoyed much worldly success,
Enter now and receive your final due process.
Your filing fee has been paid; your time here has run,
But your practice before the Heavenly Court has just begun.
The case you will forevermore handle for me,
Is to enjoy your reward throughout eternity.
You have practiced before judges and great success attained,
Now before me, your every motion will be, "Sustained."

Another very able attorney whom I have known and worked with over the years is former county attorney Gerald Holley. Gerald was the county attorney when I was took office in 1977. It took a while to get to know him because he was quiet and unobtrusive, which for some could be interpreted as being stuck-up. When you get to know Gerald, he is a very honest and straightforward attorney. He served as county attorney for over thirty years, and to my best recollection, he never lost a case. He was always available to help when I called; he gave good advice, and for many years only charged the county three hundred dollars per month retainer.

Gerald was the perfect fit as county attorney, since he lived in Washington County and had few political connections to Holmes County. He would sit in a county commissioner meeting and never say a word unless a board member asked him something. When he did speak, it was thoughtful, meaningful advice. The board usually listened to him. Gerald is a Christian and a gentleman, and that is how he practiced law. Often when someone would tell me they were going to sue the county over some issue I would tell them, "We have an attorney who has never lost a case representing us, so if you can find an attorney better than that, go ahead." We had some who tried, but none who won.

* * *

CHAPTER 10

INTERESTING CLERKS OF FLORIDA

Informal gatherings at clerks' meetings provided an entertaining diversion as we discussed some of our more colorful clerks. One of those was the late A. Curtis Powers. Known as Curtis, he was an outstanding clerk who got the job almost by accident. His political journey, as told to several of us clerks during a break in one of the clerks' meetings, goes like this: Curtis was working with a Dodge dealership in Gainesville in 1969, and business was slow. He was reading the local newspaper, which contained a story announcing the death of the Alachua County clerk of the court. Not thinking anything about the story, he went about his daily routine until his secretary told him he had a call from then governor Claude Kirk.

Curtis was a registered Republican in a predominantly Democratic County. He had supported Governor Kirk in his upset bid to be the first Republican governor of Florida since reconstruction. He took the call, and after some small talk the governor asked him if he would like to be the clerk of the circuit court of Alachua County. Curtis said he recalled wondering, "What in the heck does the clerk do?" Since car sales were slow he asked the governor what the salary was, and when the governor told him, he said his decision was easy. The salary was more that he was making selling cars, and he quickly accepted the governor's offer. One day removed from being in the dark about what a clerk did, Curtis was one. He was sworn in and began a quite colorful career as the clerk of the circuit court of Alachua County, Florida.

One of the duties of the clerk is to take the minutes of the board of county commissioners, so Curtis went to the commission meeting to take the minutes. The board had moved the clerk's nameplate and told Curtis that his services were not needed and they would take the minutes. He and the board had several more disagreements, and Curtis had to sue the board to seek relief. The case ended up before the Florida Supreme Court in the case of *Curtis Powers v. Alachua Board of County Commissioners.* The case was decided for Curtis and benefited all clerks because it set the parameters for the duties and powers for clerks until the passage of Article V years later. Curtis always said that the automobile he had furnished one of the justices to campaign on had no effect on the outcome of the case.

The late Franklin County clerk Bobby Howell combined being clerk and serving as a general in the Florida National Guard. He was clerk when the legislature removed all the clerks statewide from the old fee system of payment to a standardized salary schedule based on the size of the county. The system was set so the sheriff was the highest paid official in each county. This aggravated Bobby and he got the legislature to correct the slight he felt. Since the county operated a ferry boat to an island that was part of

Franklin County, he got his state legislator to introduce a bill paying him for being auditor and operating the county ferry. The bill was designed to make Bobby the highest-paid official in the county and was passed by the legislature and became law. Bobby said emphatically, "No elected official in Franklin County was going to make more than me." And he was correct: as long as he was clerk, he was the highest paid. Bobby served as clerk for twenty-six years and left the clerk's office in 1983 to serve as the assistant adjutant general for the state of Florida until his retirement.

One of the most interesting clerks was the Honorable Duncan Hosford, former clerk of Liberty County, Florida. Duncan was a Korean War veteran who was from the old school of honesty and integrity. He stayed in a constant battle with county commissioners over proper spending of county funds. He was a very interesting story teller, and when clerks met I would always try to find Duncan and listen to his tales from Liberty County.

The one he is best remembered for is the story of him shooting a man for trying to run over him one day. As Duncan tells the story, his family owned a large tract of land in Liberty County, and they had made somewhat of a hunting preserve for themselves and their friends to hunt and fish. Some poachers would slip in from time to time to hunt the deer, turkeys, or hogs on their preserve without permission. That was not acceptable to Duncan. He reported the incidents to the game commission, but with their limited resources they were not able to catch anybody. Duncan decided to help the game wardens, staked out the property one day, and caught some people hunting on the property illegally. He stepped out from behind a tree and told the people, who were on a four-wheel-drive jeep, to stop. The driver tried to run him over, and Duncan shot and killed the driver. The passenger jumped out and ran. Duncan called the sheriff and told him what happened. The state attorney called a grand jury and took the case before them. They returned a no true bill and agreed he was justified in the shooting.

The man's wife then sued Duncan in a civil suit, and Duncan prevailed in that suit also. He would say as he told the story that he fought Chinese and North Koreans to be free to do what he wanted to on his own land, and he was not going to let some poacher run him over.

He was reelected after the incident, and the stories did not end there. Duncan got crossed up with another elected official in the county over some issue. He said during the next election that the other official helped put a candidate in the race to try and defeat Duncan. He was out campaigning in the county one day, and three ole boys, whom he suspected his political enemies had paid to harass him, showed up. One started to use derogatory language toward Duncan, so Duncan invited him outside to finish the conversation. The altercation started out three to one, but evened up when the owner of the store, a friend of Duncan's, stepped outside and held a gun on two while Duncan dealt with the other one. Duncan and the first troublemaker went outside and had a knock-down, drag-out fight. I asked him who won, and he said, "I guess I did. I went back to campaigning the next day, and he was in the hospital." Duncan added, "The guy did not realize I was an old army infantryman when I stomped his butt."

The clerks had a meeting in Fort Lauderdale years ago in a fancy hotel with valet parking. When Duncan showed up in his pickup truck, he drove right past the valet parkers. He parked his pickup truck with valets chasing him all the way. When the head valet guy got to Duncan to explain what he had done wrong, Duncan got the first word and the last. He let the head man know quickly that none of those boys was going to get an opportunity to steal his pickup or his gun that he kept in it. The valet decided that he did not want to mess with Duncan, so every day they would just wave Duncan on through while the rest of us had to shell out the bucks and deal with the valets.

When my children were younger and would go with us to clerks' meetings, we usually had a dinner during the week with the rest of the clerks. Duncan would sit with us and entertain us with his stories. His tall tales made an impression on them. They were truly all eyes and ears when Duncan spoke, something very rare for them.

The last Duncan story I must share with you is classic. A neighbor lady had asked Duncan to keep an eye on her property, which joined his land. Duncan told her he would look out for her property like it was his own. One day late in the afternoon Duncan got a call informing him that someone was parked on the lady's property and might be poaching. Duncan grabbed his gun and went down to check on things like he had promised. He pulled up and asked the three individuals who they were and what they were doing on private property. The people, without saying a word, started the vehicle and took off. Duncan thought it was a good idea to put an exclamation mark on the situation and did so with a couple of gunshots fired up in the air and then went home. Shortly after the incident the Florida Department of Law Enforcement filed charges against Duncan. He was never arrested and the state attorney of his circuit recused himself and the governor appointed another state attorney to handle the case. The investigators came to Liberty County and interviewed countless people, including the owner of the land, who confirmed that she had asked Duncan to look after her property. She also told the investigators that the agents were on her property without her permission. The investigation also revealed that the three individuals in the car were two FDLE agents and an informant working a drug case.

When the investigation was completed the state attorney from the other circuit told the governor that Duncan had done nothing wrong. The investigation supported Duncan's story that the agents were on private property without a warrant or permission. They failed to identify themselves to Duncan when he asked and took off like thieves in the night. The state attorney refused to charge Duncan with anything and dismissed the charges that had been filed. As the case was winding down an FDLE agent asked Duncan to come by the FDLE office in Tallahassee. Duncan went by and after a rather friendly conversation the agent asked Duncan if he could see the gun that he had the night of the incident. Duncan allowed him to view the gun and the agent took off and would not return the gun to Duncan. The agent told Duncan the agency was going to ask the court to forfeit the gun to them even though Duncan was exonerated. This trick the FDLE pulled was short-lived. His attorney and nephew Ken Hosford, present day county judge in Liberty County, told the FDLE agent that he would have a hearing before the Circuit Judge if the gun was not returned. Quickly and quietly the gun was returned to Duncan. His gun was returned and his good name restored.

I have to put somewhat of a disclaimer here that states this is how I remember Duncan telling his stories. If any of the information is inaccurate, it is unintentional and I would defer to Duncan as the final word.

Duncan was finally defeated for clerk some years later but still remains a force to be reckoned with in Liberty County. Robert Hill, who recently retired as clerk in Liberty County, and I are friends and always enjoy sharing a Duncan story when we get together.

The clerk that I have been the closest to since he took office is Rickey Lyons from Lafayette County. When I first met him it was obvious we shared many of the same values and beliefs. He and his wife, Louisa, and their two children, Chad and Tori, live on a farm outside Mayo, Florida. Rickey was an FFA advisor and taught at Lafayette High School when he was elected clerk. Louisa manages the show-pig business and the family farm. It was during one of the many discussions that Rickey and I had that the idea of small county clerks owning their own software came about. We combined our ideas and money and were able to development a software package that is now called Clericus. It is running in more than half of the Florida counties.

Both Chad and Tori were state FFA officers, and that is another common bond that we enjoy. Through the years, Rickey and I have spent a great deal of time on the telephone helping each other with the constant changes that occur in the clerk's office. Rickey served as president of the clerk's association for a term. Recently he was appointed to the North Florida Community College Board of Trustees.

Martin County clerk Marsha Ewing is another clerk whom I have been friends with. She retired at the same time I did and seems to be adjusting well to retirement. Originally from Mississippi, she is a Republican, and her mom is a Democrat. That makes for some very interesting discussions. She was the president of the clerk's association when the Clericus projected started and was the first clerk from a larger county to switch to our software. I hear from her once in a while. Like Brenda and me, she is enjoying having grandchildren.

Rickey and Marsha were always just a phone call or a text away. The Florida legislature never allowed the clerks to rest on our laurels; they were constantly changing laws and procedures. Had it not been for the support we all gave each other, chances are we could not have succeeded in keeping up.

I was also close friends with Delma Allen from Desoto County and the late Coleman Best from Hardee County. Delma served for thirty-two years as clerk and never had an opponent. He retired, but eight years later his friends in the coffee shop talked him into running for county commissioner, and he won. He served four years and was defeated for reelection. I want someone to Baker Act me if I announce I want to run for county commissioner.

There were numerous other clerks whom I was friends with and who were very helpful to me. There is no way I could name them all without leaving someone out. We endured together the constant changes the legislature passed and the funding pitfalls of Article V.

Understandably I could continue with many stories of my years in the clerk's office. I have selected what I remember as the most notable court cases and other happenings that would be of interest to my readers. From this point I will take a different direction and speak from a personal standpoint relating to my family, my observations on the future of America and other things that have influenced my life.

* * *

CHAPTER 11

DEFINING INFLUENCES

EARLY YEARS

On February 15, 1949, I was born in a rental home on a small farm less than a mile from Poplar Springs High School in Holmes County, Florida. I was the second of three sons born to my parents. Sometimes I have to pinch myself and make sure that my life is not a dream that I am going to awaken from. The Lord has blessed me with a wonderful wife, four wonderful children, and so far, twelve precious grandchildren.

I was also fortunate to play on two consecutive high school state-championship basketball teams, and I averaged over thirty points per game my senior year. I was named an honorable-mention All-American high school basketball player by *Coach and Athlete Magazine* in 1967, and was elected as first vice president of the Florida Future Farmers of America. I earned a basketball scholarship at Chipola Junior College in Marianna, Florida, and at the University of West Florida in Pensacola. I won nine straight elections, the majority without opposition. I think I have been truly blessed and am thankful for the opportunities I have been given. An additional blessing came on January 6, 2009; I was sworn into office for my last term by my oldest son Zach.

North of the Mason-Dixon Line

My father had been in the Navy in World War II. After the war he returned to Holmes County to farm. At About the time he got his life adjusted he was called back into the Navy for the Korean War. When he returned, we left the farm and moved to Akron, Ohio, for him to work in the Goodyear tire and rubber plant. After a short time in Ohio my mother left my brothers and me with a baby-sitter and did not come back. When my father returned from work he loaded up everything we owned, which did not seem like much, and we headed back to Florida. He brought us to our grandparents' home and asked them to keep us for a while until he could get settled. We never knew if he came back to get us or just thought we were better off with our grandparents.

Years later my father died in Biloxi, Mississippi. He had been injured in the Korean War and drew a veteran's pension and stayed close to the VA clinic in Mississippi. He was found one day in his trailer by a neighbor, apparently having died from a heart attack. My two brothers and I went out and buried him in the VA cemetery in Biloxi. The officer in charge of the cemetery told us that in the VA cemetery the generals and the privates are treated the same. I came to realize what sacrifices many made in serving in not just one war, but two. Just like many others, it seemed to have cost him his family and the joy of seeing his children grow up. I was able to forgive him for any hard feelings I might have had when I realized how much he had gone through.

Grandparents to the Rescue

Grandparents or other family members who take grandchildren in have a special place in my heart. Daddy and Mama Register—as we called them, though they were really Rufus Cody Register and Susan Cordelia Register—had already raised nine of their own children. They took us in and never missed a beat. I was four, my older brother, Harold, was six, and my youngest brother, Terry Joe, was two. They gave us unconditional love and created a work ethic that remains today.

Daddy Register had no formal education to speak of. In the second grade he had to leave school to go to work. He could not read or write until he married Mama Register. She taught him to read and write, add and subtract. He always told us that he would pay for us to go to school as long as we wanted to, or we could follow his example and go to work. It did not take us long to understand that school was easier than the work he had planned for us. It is easy to see why the three of us finished high school and college. He was a good businessman and owned a great deal of land and several rental houses. Even though he had little formal education, he was well respected in the community. He was elected to the Holmes County School Board for a term and served several terms on the West Florida Electric Cooperative Board of Trustees.

My grandfather told us in word and by example that hard work and being trustworthy would go a long way in life. His ideas about paying debts and not owing money to anyone are still the tenets that I go by today. My wife Brenda and I did have a mortgage when we built our houses, but I never rested until we paid them off. I could hear his voice often reminding me of the costs of borrowed money.

My grandfather though that idle hands were not good for young boys. He expected us to help him build and maintain the houses he owned. We painted and repaired the houses during the summer and other breaks. When he did not have something for us to do, he found something.

He had friends who farmed and planted cotton. When we did not work for him, we picked cotton for Gene Smith or L. T. Johnson, both friends of my granddad. They would pick us up early in the morning, before daylight, along with several black men and women from Graceville. Most of the time my two brothers and me were the only white persons in the cotton field picking. L. T. Johnson's sons, Sid and Sonny, were the field bosses. They weighed the cotton and kept records of how much everybody picked. We were paid three cents per pound, and I never picked more than a hundred pounds in a day. Some of the older black men could pick three hundred pounds, and I could never figure out how they could do it. I have often thought that having all young people spend a few days in the cotton field would be beneficial in encouraging them to choose wise career paths.

Uncle Douglas Bush and his wife, Leo, one of my mother's sisters, operated a grocery store in Graceville. During the summer they let Harold and me work in the store. That is where I learned to count money and deal with the public. I loved working in the store much better than picking cotton. Uncle Doug and Aunt Leo were special to the three of us. They always made sure we got paid for working. They were the only members of my family who came to graduation at Chipola Junior College when Brenda, Harold, and I graduated. They took us out to eat at a local restaurant afterward. They are the parents of my oldest cousin, Sid Bush. Sid served in the navy and retired as a chief petty officer. We have stayed in close contact with him through the years.

I also worked for a contractor on various projects one summer. The work was hard, but looking back, it was good preparation for the future. One of my granddaddy's brothers was in the dairy business, and I worked for him one summer. Cutting and hauling silage for the cows was the main job. We worked from early morning to late in the evening. Other jobs included working for Henderson Furniture in Graceville and helping my uncle Horace Register on his farm. He allowed me some acreage to farm for a Future Farmers of America project, and in return, I plowed and helped him with his farming. One thing all these jobs had in common was that they served to motivate me to get a degree so that I might qualify for a better job.

The last attempt my granddad made to make sure that we boys had a job for the future was to encourage us to buy a farm. He thought that everyone ought to make an honest living, and farming was as good as it got for him. Harold and I were seniors at the University of West Florida when he found out about a farm and a dairy that were for sale. We visited both and quickly decided that we did not want to be in the dairy business. An older couple wanted to sell their farm so they could move to Texas to be near their children. The farm contained 121 acres along with the farmhouse and all the farm equipment. I negotiated the final price of $19,750. We went to Graceville, completed the paperwork, and Daddy Register loaned us the money to buy the land. We were glad to be big landowners and not even out of college. My granddad added a verbal stipulation that we would have to offer Terry Joe forty acres at the same price we paid for it.

We paid Daddy Register every penny back including interest. It made him so happy to see us be able to make the payments—not that he needed the money, but it proved to him that he had taught us a lesson about being responsible enough to repay a loan. When

Brenda and I decided to build closer to where we both worked, we sold our part of the farm to Harold and built our first house near Bonifay. We never became farmers, but the land was a nice investment that helped all of us in starting our lives.

I find myself going back almost daily and thinking of things my granddad told me about life and how to deal with life. He told me once that you could judge a man by his enemies as well as his friends. At the time the statement meant nothing to me, but as the years went by I began to understand. It came to me in the middle of one of my campaigns what he meant when certain people were out trying to defeat me. It was as plain as the nose on my face. Since then, I have thought many times that you can judge a man or woman better by their enemies than their friends. I wish I had taken more opportunities to thank him for all he and my grandmother did for me.

My grandmother, Susan Cordelia Tindell Register, had a dark complexion, and a relative told me that her mother was part Native American. Two of my children are dark complexioned, and we often told them the story of their grandmother, who died before they were born. My daughter, Hilary, who graduated in 2008 from the University of Florida College of Dental Medicine, asked me about being eligible for scholarships for being part Native American. A local historian in our county claimed to have the necessary documentation proving my children and I were part Native American, but we never followed through on the idea.

My grandmother made sure we knew about God and knew how to pray. We prayed before each meal, and our grandparents took us to church regularly. If they could not go we went with one our uncles. We went to a little Baptist church in the county and loved the fellowship that it provided. All three of us were baptized at an early age, accepting the Lord as our savior. Mama Register played the piano and required us to sing as she played. Consequently we memorized most of the songs in the Baptist hymnal. Even today those songs come back to me at various times. Every family gathering always included a special time when everyone would gather around the piano and sing. We had to sing before we could go outside and play football or basketball. We did not have a television set in our house until I was in middle school, so singing or playing helped us pass the time. We did not have air conditioning or even a fan until years later. In the summer we just let the windows up and prayed for a breeze. Christmas presents were usually clothes, shoes, and fruit. One Christmas, however, my grandfather bought me a doctor's kit with a stethoscope and other doctor items. He told me he got it for me because he knew I was going to be a doctor or a preacher because I never wanted to go barefooted in the summer like most other children did.

My grandmother had an abundance of old sayings that she used in her conversations each day. They come back to me often when faced with certain situations. The worst thing I ever heard her say about anyone was that he was "sorry as gully dirt." Those of us who grew up around gullies know that at the topsoil is washed away and all that is left is clay and nothing will grow; hence, it is good for nothing. She had another saying regarding the weather that said if March "comes in like a lion, it goes out like a lamb, and if it comes in like a lamb it goes out like a lion." I think of her every March as I look to see which one wins out, the lamb or lion.

My grandparents owned a couple hundred acres of land on the west side of Graceville, Florida. The property contained a nice pond called Collins Old Mill Pond. One of my uncles, Lloyd Register, ran a grist mill that ground cornmeal. The pond was the beginning of Holmes Creek. As boys we helped run the business by helping with the manufacturing and delivery of the cornmeal. The creek started on Daddy Register's land and continued through Vernon, Florida, to the Choctawhatchee River in Washington County. This creek was a perfect playground for three young boys and their friends. My grandfather allowed us to go swimming about any time we wanted—that is, when we were not working. We fished, camped, and had a wonderful time being the Tom Sawyers of Graceville, Florida. It was a miracle we survived the snakes, swimming by ourselves, and all the other things we did on that creek. My grandmother would say we were under the hand of God.

My granddad lived to the ripe old age of ninety-two, and when he died he had a respectable estate for one from such humble beginnings. His children, one of whom was my mother, argued over the estate until everything was finally sold and the money divided. It saddened me to see the property leave the family. It held many fond childhood memories for my two brothers and me.

Having such a broad area to freely roam and enjoy seemed to make up for the fact that we never had a bicycle or a BB gun or many other things that some boys and girls had. Being able to be outside, to fish and hunt and camp out when we wanted to, more than made up for the things that we did not have. Children today probably spend too much time in front of a television or computer. Health wise they need to spend more time outdoors.

To begin my education my grandfather brought me to Poplar Springs School in the fall of 1954 to meet my first-grade teacher. My teacher was Mrs. Adele Corbett; I thought she was one of the prettiest ladies I had ever seen. She was a great teacher. She taught us the basics of reading, writing, and arithmetic. School was fun for me, and I made good grades. There was never a question at our home about going to school every day. It was a standard rule; if you were sick enough to miss school you probably needed a dose of castor oil. Just the thought of taking the terrible-tasting oil earned me perfect attendance certificates year after year.

Two-Time State Champs

Another event took place in 1956 that would have a profound effect on my future. The Holmes County School Board decided it was time to build a gymnasium at our school and replace the dirt court. The first basketball game we played in elementary school was played outside, using an old garbage can with the bottom out hung over a stump for the goal. The basketball was a pine cone. The gym was finished when I was in the sixth grade. The coach, L. T. Johnson, was so proud of the new gym that any student who stepped on the gym floor without tennis shoes automatically got a whipping with his belt. It was funny to watch. We would tiptoe around the edge of the court to make sure we did not become the object of Coach Johnson's wrath.

The county tourney was played in our gym when I was in the sixth grade. The tournament had a junior team division made up of seventh, eighth, and ninth graders. Poplar Springs was playing Prosperity, a small school that only went through eighth grade. At halftime we were so far ahead that Coach Johnson called for several of us sixth graders to play in the second half. The jerseys were so big the armpits went all the way to our waist, but we were so proud to get to play. None of us had tennis shoes, so the first game I played for the Poplar Springs High School Atomics, I was barefooted as a yard dog. I scored six points against the Prosperity team.

I loved the competition that basketball afforded, and I excelled in later years, becoming what many considered a good player. Sadly,

Coach Johnson died of a heart attack a couple of years later. His twin sons, Ronnie and Donnie, were a year behind me in school. We played on the basketball team together. His oldest son, L. T. (Sonny Johnson), was my junior varsity basketball team coach, and we were undefeated for that season.

In 1964 Herman Dodson was hired as the new head basketball coach at Poplar Springs. My sophomore year I played on the varsity and we had a break-even season. My brother Harold was a senior, so we got to play one year of varsity ball together. In a grudge match with arch-rival Graceville High School, he and I together scored over sixty points to help the Atomics win. I averaged twenty-four points a game, and people were really looking forward to the next season, hoping that we might have a chance to win the school's first state tournament.

Poplar Springs High School had a long and proud tradition of good basketball teams but had never managed to win a state tournament. It was growing up and hearing of this tradition that made me and my peers set a goal to win a state tournament for the school. We practiced often and kept the gym open almost constantly through the summer months. I have seldom seen a group of boys who were so dedicated to a common cause. We discussed the championship often and dedicated ourselves to the team concept of preparing to win. The 1966 year started very well for us. We had a good team, and with a few stumbles along the way we got better as the season went along. By tournament time we were in high gear and there was no stopping us. The run-and-gun offense blew away the competition with ease, and before we knew it we were in the state championship game at the University of Florida gym.

We had a great team effort, and I averaged twenty-six points a game for the year as we won the school's first state championship.

We began my senior year with great expectations. We started the season in Grand Ridge and lost in a close game. So much for respecting the state champs.

Before Christmas of my senior year I had a family tragedy that would change my life forever. December 13, 1966, I arrived home from school—Poplar Springs High School, just outside of Graceville, Florida. The phone was ringing. I answered it, and the voice on the other end of the line asked me how old I was. I told the lady I was seventeen. The caller told me that my grandfather, Mr. Rufus Register Sr., and his wife, my grandmother, Susan Register, had been in an automobile accident and that someone in the family needed to come and sign paperwork for the needed surgery for my grandfather. I asked her about my grandmother, and she would not answer. I called one of my aunts to go with me to Marianna, Florida, where my grandfather was in the hospital. Just outside of Marianna we came upon the wreck site on Highway 90. It was a mess, a head-on between a drunk driver and my grandparents. We stopped and looked at the wreck, and someone told me my grandmother had died at the scene. We went on to the hospital, and the nurses allowed me to sign the surgical permission forms for my grandfather. He survived the wreck and the surgery, but he never walked again without the assistance of a walker.

Two days later, on the same day my grandmother was buried, I scored fifty-three points in a basketball game in the county tournament. The Lord gave me the peace of mind to play, and the memory of my grandmother seemed to inspire me on every play. The events of that week showed me how quickly one's world could be turned upside down.

We went on to post a 32-2 record and held on to our state title. I averaged over thirty points a game for the year. We were very fortunate to have a tall team for the sixties. Doyle Holland and Bo Creel were both six foot five. Gerald Hayes was six foot four, and I was six foot two. The Johnson twins, Ronnie and Donnie, were both over six feet. I owe so much of the personal success I enjoyed to these guys. Benny Joe Bell was our point guard on the 1967 team. Dewitt Scott was the point guard on the 1966 team. Benny Joe and Dewitt always guarded the other team's best outside shooter and were always ready to give an assist. It was easy to be a star on a team with such unselfish players. I do not get to see these guys much anymore. The school had a forty-year reunion in 2007, and most of them were there. It was so good to see them again. We all will remember to our dying day that great feeling of victory at Florida Gym on the campus of the University of Florida two years in a row.

As we were preparing for the 1967 state tournament, Coach Dodson arranged for us to go down to Holmes County High School to practice on their new glass backboards. The backboards we had were the old fan-shaped ones and Florida Gym had the glass backboards. As we were practicing in the Holmes County High gym I noticed a pretty cheerleader named Brenda Garrett. My older brother Harold was dating a girl from Bonifay who happened to be friends with Brenda, and one night when she came by to see my brother, she brought Brenda with her. We sat on the front porch in the swing. We were having our first conversation, and the chain that held the swing broke and she fell over on me, and the rest is history. We started dating, and as an indication of her tenacious spirit, she hitched a ride to the state tournament in 1967 with a friend of the family. She went to the state tournament to cheer me on. Her mom agreed for her to go only because her brother, Lowell Garrett, was in pharmacy school at the University of Florida and she could stay with him.

Chipola Years

My senior year I decided to accept a scholarship to play basketball with Chipola Junior College in Marianna, Florida. I had several offers from other schools, including four-year schools, but decided to stay close to home. Brenda also went to Chipola and was selected as a cheerleader for the Indians; we spent two wonderful years in Marianna. Since neither of us had an automobile we either walked or hitched a ride everywhere.

At Chipola I roomed with Jerry Davis, a basketball player from Crestview. He had a car, and I would help him buy gas, so he would get us to school and basketball practice. Brenda rode the bus from Bonifay to Marianna each day, a distance of about thirty miles one way. Some nights she would stay in the girls' dorm with some of the other cheerleaders if we had a game. College life suited us both well; we made good grades, even though mine were not as good as Brenda's.

Coach Johnson was great coach, and I enjoyed my two years with him. I kept up with him through the years and returned in 2008 when the college had a reunion for all his ball players. My oldest son, Zach, who played for Coach Johnson in 1992, was able to attend the reunion with me. Zach and I were one of the only two father-son combinations who played for Coach Johnson. Coach Johnson was in his eighties and a little frail but still had a gleam in his eye. Not many people influenced the number of young people that he did, and I am forever grateful for his example. Hilary later played for Chipola for two years, and as far as I know, Zach, Hilary, and I are the only father-son-daughter combination to all play for the Indians.

Chipola Junior College was a good transition from Mill Creek Road in Graceville, Florida, and Poplar Springs High School. It was small, and the students always got the attention they needed. I am not sure I would have made it had I been thrown into a large four-year school to begin with.

When Jeb Bush was elected governor, a friend of mine who had worked in his campaign called me one day. He wanted to know if I thought Brenda would be interested in serving on the board of trustees for Chipola. I told him I would check with her, and she agreed. She was appointed and served ten years on the board. She served as chairperson in 2005. During her time on the board, Chipola athletic teams were very successful. The girls' softball and boys' baseball teams won national championships. We were able to attend the Boys' National Baseball Tournament in Grand Junction, Colorado, with Chipola president Dr. Gene Prough and his wife, Priscilla. It was the fiftieth anniversary of junior college baseball. Many of the Chipola faithful enjoyed being on hand for this first national baseball championship. We also attended several boys' and girls' national basketball tournaments in Hutchinson and Salina, Kansas.

Coach Johnson died on February 13, 2009, two days before my sixtieth birthday. I went to his viewing and paid my respects to his family. With his passing, and the fact that I reached sixty years of age made me realize that time moves on and waits for no one.

UWF and The Draft

Thankfully, I signed a basketball scholarship agreement after Chipola to play basketball at the University of West Florida. Brenda attended also and was on the cheerleading squad. We spent two enjoyable years in Pensacola. My brother Harold was there with Brenda and me. We shared a Ford Mustang that our granddad loaned us the money to buy. He and I graduated from UWF and became, as far as I know, the first in our family to graduate from college.

When I graduated from UWF in the spring of 1971, the Vietnam War was going on, and my draft number was eighty-nine. My deferment lasted only until I graduated from college. I immediately received my notice to report for my physical in Montgomery, Alabama. It appeared I was about to be inducted into the army. I traveled by bus from Marianna, Florida, and passed my physical. I had already applied to the Florida National Guard, but all the local units were full.

I got a phone call one day in Pensacola from a family friend who worked for the Florida National Guard in Panama City, Florida. He told me they had had some openings and if I could get to Panama City that day he could get me in the guard. Brenda and I had planned our wedding for June and thought we might have to postpone it if I went into the army. Fortunately, I was able to go to Panama City that day and was sworn into the Florida National Guard, Panama City Unit. I was told by the guard personnel not to worry, that I would not have to go to basic training until after my wedding in June.

During the next guard drill they told me I was headed to Fort Polk, Louisiana, on April 22, 1971. This was the first time I realized how good Brenda was at adjusting to a life of uncertainty. We just decided to go ahead and get married before I went. She changed the dates on the wedding invitations and sent them out. We were married on Sunday night, April 18, 1971, after the regular Sunday-night service at the First Baptist Church of Bonifay. With a little rearranging, we had a simple wedding and reception, with our families and friends taking part. I had to leave the next Thursday morning for Fort Polk, Louisiana, for basic training.

Looking back on it, basic training was a good experience, but at the time, it was rough. The summer of 1971 was hot in Fort Polk. Brenda had to encourage me to hang in there, and I graduated from basic training in August of 1971. I was awarded the "trainee of the cycle" award for the company.

After basic training I rode home in the back of a pickup truck from Fort Polk to Bonifay. Lamar Edenfield, from Altha, a boy I had played basketball against in high school, had a truck and offered me a ride. Brenda picked me up at Simbo's restaurant in Bonifay, and we went to Panama City, Florida. She had gotten her first job teaching at Jenks Junior High in Bay County and had rented us an apartment in St. Andrews, a section of Panama City, Florida.

Finally, a Job

Patience was never one of my virtues, and the process of looking for a job was discouraging.. After several unsuccessful interviews and Brenda reminding me that the Lord had a job for me, things turned around. Beverly Helms, a school administrator in Washington County, Florida, and a friend who had attended the same high school as me, called one day and told me that Department of Transportation had some job openings. She told me that she had a friend whose husband, was an assistant district right-of-way agent, so she had put in a good word for me. I went to Chipley and applied for the position of right-of-way agent. Interstate 10 was being built, and the DOT was hiring several agents to buy the right of way. I went for an interview and a few days later I got notified that I had the job. I started shortly thereafter. I spent almost two years with The Florida Department of Transportation buying right of way.

Since we were both now employed, Brenda and I bought a 1971 Toyota Corolla for $2,000. Daddy Register loaned us the money, and we kept the car until we had children. The car was a floor shift, had no air, and had an AM-FM radio. Brenda and I went on our first vacation to the mountains in it and had a wonderful time.

I would also be remiss if I did not mention that I learned through much unnecessary worry that God always provides a way. If I had listened to Brenda I could have been spared much of the worry. After a couple of years I got an opportunity to go to work for the University of Florida Extension Service in Holmes County as an assistant county agent 4-H coordinator. I went to work there in 1973. The job required me to organize 4-H clubs throughout the county and work with young people. I had horse clubs, livestock clubs, and general-purpose clubs. Little did I know at the time that dealing with young people from every school in the county was building a strong political base for the future.

Brenda, at this time, was expecting our first child and working as a guidance counselor at two different schools in the county, Bethlehem and Poplar Springs. In March of 1974 our first son, Zachary Brent Taylor, was born. My life, at that point, was forever changed.

I worked with the Extension for two more years, and in the spring of 1976 I got my first inclination to run for office. The county agent for Holmes County at that time was Bo Taylor, no kin to me, but a very nice man who raised walking horses in his spare time. Brenda was expecting our second child at this time. She and I were at a

4-H horse show in Ponce de Leon, Florida, when she told me she was going into labor. After some rushing around, Whitney Jacob Taylor was born shortly after midnight, April 4, 1976.

A Man and His Music

In addition to my children and grandchildren's influence on my life music has also been an influence. You can tell a great deal about a person by the type music they listen to. Growing up all we had in the home was a radio. Our favorite radio station was WBAM, Montgomery, Alabama. The station played a cross between country and rock and roll. They signed off each day at five o'clock. Later on I became mostly a country music fan until around forty, and then oldies from the fifties and sixties became my music of choice. Some of these songs are etched in my mind so vividly. I now have satellite radio and can listen to the oldies and easy instrumentals exclusively if I want.

Music has always been special since my grandmother Register played the piano for my two brothers and me to sing all the gospel greats. Music has provided some of my most memorable experiences in church. Some of Vern Gosdin's music really touches my soul. Don Williams and Elvis Presley sing many of my favorites as well. Elvis's gospel music, to me, is some of his greatest work. Brenda and I have always loved the Beach Boys and have always wanted to see them in concert. Anne Murray and Olivia Newton John are two female performers we have always enjoyed. Since I have retired I listen to easy instrumentals and have come to love the music of Floyd Cramer. Music speaks a language, tells a story, takes you to a place or time, and expresses the content of your heart and soul, like no other medium can.

Hilary made me promise if Dwight Yokum came anywhere close I would take her to the concert. A couple of years before she left the University of Florida she called one day and told me he was going to be in Jacksonville at the Florida Theater. I called to get tickets, and the three of us went. It was a great concert. The smaller venue gave us the feeling of having a more personal contact with the artist and enhanced the sound quality.

My hearing is starting to diminish, so in a civic center setting, the volume increase is very uncomfortable to me. When we went to see George Strait at the Tallahassee Civic Center, I had to wear ear plugs.

* * *

CHAPTER 12

My Children

I could not write my memories without telling about my children and how they fit into the political process. Our oldest son, Zachary Brent, was born in 1974, Whitney Jacob in 1976, Lucas Nathaniel in 1978, and Hilary Jordan in 1981. The only life they have ever known is being the children of a public official. They handled it as well as any children could have. When we had our first son, Zach, I did not know how we could love anyone as much as we loved him. When Whit came along I found out how you can love another child—the Lord gives you a greater capacity to love. We have seen that happen with each of our children and our grandchildren.

Brenda's mother, Eula Garrett, was our in-home babysitter. She came to our house and kept every one of the children until they started to school. She was a sweet Christian lady who raised Brenda and two boys, Gerald and Lowell, having lost a third son at age seven in an accident. She worked in a local department store in town, making very little money. The boys both went into the navy, and

Brenda was born to her later in life. Brenda's dad died when she was a young girl, and Mrs. Garrett had the challenging job of raising a daughter alone. Mrs. Garrett had red hair and would have loved to have lived long enough to see Hilary's little redheaded boy, Taylor, as well as all the other grandchildren.

Mrs. Garrett read to the boys and later to Hilary every day and did a wonderful job of babysitting three mischievous boys and a little girl. The only downside to her babysitting was that she was an avid soap opera fan. So her grandchildren had a front-row seat to *As the World Turns* and *The Young and the Restless* every day. We often kidded her about it, but she took the kidding in stride. She died at the age of eighty-eight, and all the grandchildren love to retell some Grandma Eula stories when we get together as a family.

Very often as little ones my kids would come by the courthouse and play, waiting on me to get off. They would watch trials and see the criminals brought to court as well as other happenings at the courthouse. The newspaper editor would call every now and then to inform me that he had just seen four children jump off the ledge of the courthouse onto a grassy spot below. They never got hurt and finally grew out of the desire to jump.

Thankfully my children were generally well behaved and caused us very few problems. We took them to the church nursery when they were a couple of weeks old and church attendance was part of their life. The children played baseball, soccer, football, and basketball. Zach and Hilary both played basketball at Chipola College. Whit scored the first three-point shot in the new Holmes County High gym. Luke led his team to the county basketball championship and played golf also. Three of the four children worked at the local Piggly Wiggly food store. It provided a realistic look at life working and dealing with the public. All of them worked as lifeguards at the local recreational center during the summers. Their work experience allowed them to learn a great deal about people and life.

None of the children had an automobile until they needed one in college. Zach spent his first semester at Chipola without a car. He had worked at the Piggy Wiggly and had saved around $4,000 and wanted to buy his first car. I told him to go ahead. He went down to the local dealership and picked out a red Camaro. He came by the courthouse and told me that I needed to go down and sign for him to get the car. I told him I was going to do him a favor by not doing that. He went home a little miffed and told his mom. She did exactly what she needed to do—she supported me. The next day he went back to the dealer and made arrangements to buy a white Corsica with payments that he could handle.

He continued to work at the Piggy Wiggly, made his car payments, and attended Florida State University, Panama City branch, to finish his degree. He even had his own gas account at a local store and paid for his own gas. When he went to law school in Jackson, Mississippi, we made his payments until he graduated. He did remind me that I was harder on him than the other children, because I never made any of them pay for the things he did. He married a Jacksonville girl, Jana Spurling. They have three children: a daughter, Jordan Michelle; our first grandson, Jacob Lee; and in 2011 they added another son, Jackson Garrett. Zach started his legal career in the state attorney's office, and after several years there, associated with the firm of Manuel and Thompson.

In the fall of 1995, Whit registered to take the pharmacy school entrance exam at Pensacola Junior College in Pensacola. The testing service had sent him a notice telling him where the test would be administered. Brenda went with him, as she did with all the children on test days. They took great pains to get a hotel room near the test site so that test morning would be minimally stressful. They arrived at the college and located the building where the test was supposed to be administered, but no one was there. The testing site had been changed. Whit did not get the notification through the mail or by phone like the others taking the test. It took them some time to find the testing room. Even the janitorial staff working that day had no idea where the test was being administered. When they arrived, the testing had already begun. The lady in charge told Brenda and Whit that no one could start the test late and that he would have to reschedule. Brenda let the lady know that Whit had not been notified of the change in location. She informed her that they had been searching the campus for over an hour and asked that she call the testing service to get permission for special testing conditions under the circumstances. Thankfully the lady reluctantly agreed to call the testing service. The service agreed to make a special exception for Whit to take the exam with a proctor in another room. Chances are if he had been alone he would have returned home without taking the test. He did very well on the exam and got into the University of Florida School of Pharmacy. This incident has given the family many laughs about how persistent Brenda is when it comes to her children.

We loaded Whit up and took him to Archer Road, the main drag of the University of Florida. He was there for the next four years, and Luke, Brenda, and I moved him several times. It was at the University of Florida that he met his wife, Shellie Bishop. They have four of our grandchildren: Kodie Lynn named after her grandpa; Campbell Reese; and the twins, Graham Michael and Gwynneth Grace. Kodie is the first grandchild to test the political waters. She was elected vice president of her school's student government.

Whit is a supervising pharmacist with Publix. We visited them over New Year's holiday, 2009, and Campbell, who was around four years old, said to me, "Grandpa, did you get a haircut?" I told her yes, and I leaned over for her to get a closer look and asked her how she liked it. She touched me on my bald spot and said, "Grandpa... they cut a hole in it!" That's pretty observant for a four-year-old. She let me know there is always another way of looking at things.

Luke attended Chipola College and FSU Panama City branch and then law school in Jackson, Mississippi, at Mississippi College School of Law. He actually moved back in with us for over a year after he graduated from law school, the only one of our children to do so. It was a wonderful time for his mom and me. He bought a house in town, and Brenda and I, along with Meg, his bride to be, worked on the house for a year. Brenda and I went on a trip to Orlando in November of that year, and when we returned home he had moved into his new house. It almost killed his mom to have the last child leave home.

He worked with the state attorney's office for two years and opened his own practice in July of 2006. He married a local girl, Meghan Spear, and they live in Bonifay and are the proud parents of grandchild number eight, a fine boy named Elijah Lucas, and grandchild number twelve, baby Abram James.

I had the honor of swearing both Zach and Luke into the practice of law, in the courtroom of the Holmes County courthouse. It has been rewarding to watch my sons in hearings and during trials. Sometimes I think the dream of going to law school myself is being lived out through my sons. Luke is a part-time assistant state attorney in addition to running his private practice. Brenda and I went with Luke to Tampa to take the Florida Bar. After two days of test taking I asked him how he did; his reply was, "Let's get out of here." We had to wait six weeks to find out the results. He had to pass three different sections, and it was great to see that glorious word, "PASS," in three different places beside his name.

Hilary attended Chipola Junior College just like the rest of our family. She played basketball there, becoming the third member of our family to do so. She then went to the University of Florida and earned her undergraduate degree before being accepted into dental school at UF. For one year between undergrad and dental school she worked for the Oral Biology Department in the Periodontal Disease Research Center as a research assistant. Working that year helped her mature and be ready for the daunting task of dental school.

Hilary graduated from the University of Florida College of Dentistry in May of 2008. She married a local boy, Wesley Whitaker, and they reside on Malcolm Taylor Road in the county. They have a son, Taylor Wesley, a daughter, Brighton Claire, and their latest addition is sweet Georgia Brynn, born in 2012. Hilary began her dental career with Family Dentistry with offices in Bonifay and Chipley on June 2, 2008. All three of the boys were on hand for her graduation in Gainesville. It was quite a family celebration. Her graduation ended sixteen straight years of Brenda and me having someone in college. Six of those years we had three in college at one time. We often said that the condo in Destin, which we never bought, was invested instead in our children's education. We also have agreed that we have no regrets and give God the glory for how he blessed us all the way.

To be honest, I almost miss the days of getting the calls from Hilary which began with, "Daddy, I need a favor." The favor was how much money I needed to put in her checking account. I have noticed my account has grown nicely since her graduation.

Brenda is now babysitting for Hilary and Luke, something she said she was not going to do. Hilary talked her into keeping little Taylor Whitaker for a couple of months. A couple of months have become five years, and we have added four more to the daycare. Brenda announced to me that she was going to keep them until the swine flu subsided. Apparently the epidemic still rages. We are reminded once again of the power and majesty of our Creator and Heavenly Father each time one of these beautiful, precious babies is born into our family. We are so humbly grateful.

In 1995 the kids were all about to leave home; the boys bought Brenda a beautiful registered female Labrador retriever puppy. She registered her with the American Kennel Club as Ruby Lee-Tay and called her Ruby. She was instrumental in helping her make that transition when our children left home. Ruby had two litters of puppies, and Brenda kept one female pup from each litter. From the first she kept the only chocolate female of the litter, and named her Taylor's Mocha Finesse, Finny for short. From Ruby's last litter she kept a black female she named Velma's Voodoo Vixen. Finny was large, beautiful, and very athletic as evidenced by her tennis ball obsession and water retrieval. She was big, but she was so gentle and humble, and could be easily bullied by the selfish, bossy little Vixen or the strict mama Ruby any time. She was the perfect mother dog; she had several litters, and the pups were fine, healthy dogs. Brenda spent a great deal of time with each of those puppies during the eight weeks they were with her. She played with and handled them for socialization purposes, getting them accustomed to humans so they would adapt well to the families they went to. She almost did a home study before she would sell anyone a pup. She had to feel assured that the love and care she gave them would be continued in their new home.

Getting older was taking its toll on Ruby, and Finny developed cancer and died at age eleven. Eventually, Ruby would follow. On March 1, 2010, at age fifteen, Ruby was having a hard time getting up, and I called Dr. Brad Johnson, Brenda's cousin. He told us that she was failing and would not get better. As her condition worsened, we decided to allow him to put her down. I buried Ruby beside Finny. Vixen, our last Lab, died on June 12, 2010. She had been diagnosed with heart worms and had just begun the treatments. Brenda went out to give her the meds and found her dead. It seemed after her mother died she just seemed to lose the will to live. She was the only one who had never been alone. I buried her alongside her mama and sister. Losing a family animal is never easy. They were like family and brought so much to our lives when that nest began to empty. Brenda is convinced that God knew and provided just what she needed to bridge the gap during that difficult time of family transition and loss. They taught us a lot about life...things you might never expect to learn from a dog.

Having our grandchildren come along has made it a little easier to adjust to their absence in our lives. I sent the boys an e-mail telling them that the kindness they showed their mom back in 1995 had had quite an impact on many people. Of course the family loved the dogs, but many families who took one of the pups into their home benefited by getting a great new family member too. Our buyers would tell others where they got their pups so we often got calls asking if we had any more pups for sale. I told Brenda one day that I wished she loved me the way she loved those Labs. She told me if I loved her the way they did, she would. They were always glad to see you, never mad at you, held no grudges, and were willing to accept any attention you could spare. They taught us so much about life, relationships, and in reality, how we should be... loyal, joyful, forgiving, able to enjoy the moment, and capable of giving unconditional love. Brenda has a small bone-shaped sign in our home that reads, "The average dog is a nicer person than the average person." There is a lot of truth in that.

* * *

CHAPTER 13

CHANGING OF THE GUARD

I have noticed as I get older that people look at me differently. I saw this difference in the eyes of jurors. Before I retired, jurors looked at me with a kind and respectful look as if to say, "He has been here a long time, and his hair is graying; he must know what he is doing." I appreciated every group of jurors and their commitment to the judicial system. I savored every moment, realizing what a blessing I had been given in serving as clerk.

Being clerk for many years taught me that right and wrong are many times hard to distinguish. When I first took office I thought all decisions would be black and white. In reality, however, many things you deal with are in the gray area. A public official must have a good moral compass in order to make the right decisions. Ironically, many answers to problems are not found in the law. Sometimes common sense and a good conscience must provide the answer. My faith and prayer helped me make the right decisions and at times helped me get over having made the wrong ones.

Most officeholders will admit that some of the frankest conversations they have ever had have been with themselves. Having a wife for a sounding board was always helpful to me through troubled times. A supportive network of fellow clerks is also a huge plus. Many times a call to another clerk gave me the guidance I needed. A good staff is also invaluable in helping make logical, commonsense decisions that stand the test of time.

I have noticed the changing of the guard in the community. There is not one attorney who is practicing law in Holmes County who was practicing here when I became clerk in January of 1977. I have seen the entire local bar association change. When I retired, all the old attorneys had passed on. The next generation had replaced them, and some of them have passed on. My son Luke is one of the new young attorneys now practicing in Holmes County.

Businesses that were flourishing during the early years of my time in office have closed or changed hands. Mr. Carl Ingram owned and operated the Western Auto store on Waukesha Street for many years. He supplied many of the families of Bonifay with a local place to buy many of the items necessary in a home, like furniture, appliances, and lawn and garden products. He was also the go-to man at Christmas for toys and bicycles for local families who did most of their shopping in town. He would allow people to buy over time, since many families could not afford to make home purchases right out. He passed the store along to his son, Shawn, who later closed the store and sold the building to a man interested in using it for a worship center.

Several years back, a local business, Son's Tire Center, changed owners when Son retired after forty years in the tire business. Son Chance was one of the most respected businessmen in Holmes County. I began doing business with him when I first moved to

Bonifay. He was a Christian man whom you could rely on to deal honestly with you. I bought many sets of tires from him, and he allowed me pay him by the month. Brenda and I operated on a tight budget with four children. It was especially difficult when we had so many in colleges at one time and so many vehicles on the road. I knew it would be a sad day when he retired, and it was. Change is inevitable, but sometimes you trick yourself into thinking that things will stay the same. It was easy to think that as long as Son Chance was running Son's Tire Center down there on Waukesha, just north of the railroad track, all was right with the world. Oh well, I guess that is why Son's retirement affected me the way it did. Larry Cook, a young businessman, bought Son's Tire Center, has taken over, and does a good job. Now I do business with Larry.

The day Howell Chevrolet Company closed in 2007 was another sad day for our community. George Howell Sr. and his son, George Ed Howell, operated the Chevrolet dealership for over fifty years. Most of the vehicles we owned came from them, including our first conversion van. Brenda and I had seen the Tugaloo River conversion vans on one of our trips and told George Ed Howell about them. He contacted the company and became a dealer for them. A community is never the same when it loses its only new car dealership.

Lawrence Cloud has operated Cloud Auto Parts for many years, and he has always been a close friend of mine. He is a testament to how a local parts business can compete with the chain stores. Once when Zach was returning to law school in Jackson, Mississippi, he had an alternator failure in Pensacola on a Sunday afternoon. He called just before church time and told me what had happened. I called Lawrence, and we met at the auto parts store and collected the parts we needed to repair the car. He knew I would never be able to do the work myself, so he offered to go with me. We went to Pensacola, and it took Lawrence and a friend of Zach's, who was riding to school with him, just a few minutes to install the alternator. The trip to Pensacola and back was most enjoyable.

Lawrence was always a good conversationalist and great humorist. He built a parts business on the basis of his honesty and the fact that people liked him and wanted to do business with him. Even when the chain parts store came to town it did not bother Lawrence. They might have had auto parts for sale, but they could not provide the humor, the entertainment, and the view of life that you could get at Cloud's Auto Parts. When Hilary was young and losing her baby teeth, she did not like for anyone to bother them, but she would always let Lawrence. He had an easy way of extracting those little teeth, so she did not mind letting him help her. When she graduated from dental school he told her that he had been her dentist up until now but it was time for her to return the favor.

Lawrence related another humorous story concerning another businessman in the community. A local used car dealer who was known for being a little aggravating at times walked into the parts store one day, so Lawrence, in his friendly manner, asked him how he was doing. The used car guy said, "Why do you care, are you a doctor?" Lawrence responded, never missing a beat, "No, I am a veterinarian, and I know a horse's behind when I see one." The used car salesman just laughed and went on his way.

In March of 2009, after all his years in business, Lawrence decided to get involved in city politics. He ran for city council and was elected unopposed. He now brings some much needed humor to the council meetings. Luke is the city attorney and testifies to the fact that Lawrence keeps the meetings lively. Even though he is in his seventies, he seems so much younger when you see him and talk to him. He is proof that a positive attitude and a great sense of humor can go a long way in helping keep a person young. After a term on the council, the mayor retired and Lawrence ran for and was elected mayor, unopposed.

Even a bad health report could not quell Lawrence's sense of humor. I asked him how he was doing, and his response was classic Lawrence. He said the doctor had given him six months unless he didn't pay the doctor bill, then he would have six more. He concluded by saying, "You know, I might not even pay that bill."

* * *

CHAPTER 14

ORGANIZATIONS

I joined the First Baptist Church shortly after Brenda and I married, and we have been active members since. Our children were raised in the church and all were baptized accepting Jesus as their savior. I have been a deacon for many years and served in other capacities too. In recent years I have been the moderator for the church and treasurer. I was also the Royal Ambassador director for many years while my boys were growing up. Royal Ambassadors is the mission organization for boys in the Baptist church.

I went to a mission training held by the Florida Baptist Church some years ago, and during the meeting the man conducting the event mentioned that there were lay mission opportunities for families. When I got home I mentioned it to Brenda. We decided that since we had already taken the children to Disney World, Sea World, and Six Flags, we should make the next summer trip a family mission trip. I checked with the Florida Baptist mission folks, and they had just what we needed. Florida Baptist had partnered with the Montana Baptists and were sponsoring a week-long pastors' retreat at a camp in the Rocky Mountains, where local pastors could come for training and renewal. While the pastors met, their families would have access to various programs for different age groups; Royal Ambassadors for the boys, Girls' Auxiliary for the girls, Mission Friends for preschoolers, and a nursery for babies. Lay mission workers were needed to staff the camps, and families could go along. We signed up along with several others from the Holmes Baptist Association and the time we spent in the beautiful surroundings working with the Montana church families was a blessing.

The next summer the group was offered a mission trip to Mechanicsburg, Pennsylvania. To be honest, Southern Baptists had a big challenge reaching people in Pennsylvania. We conducted a sports camp for young people, and Brenda and the ladies organized backyard vacation bible schools. In addition, some others worked to remodel an old church, which had housed worshippers from both sides during the Civil War. All of our children took part in the activities. The children all went knocking on doors and handing out flyers providing information about the events that were being offered. During the activities the leaders shared the love of Jesus with those present.

The organization that I most enjoyed through the years was the Holmes County Fair Association. The reason the fair association was such a great group to work with was that all the members were volunteers. The group worked together for the common good of the county. I first learned about the Holmes County Fair as a high school student participating in the public speaking contest through my FFA chapter. When I became the assistant county agent in 1973 I became an active member of the association. I recruited Don Sallas, one of my 4-H volunteers, who later became the fair secretary and manager. He was active for over thirty years and was the heart and soul of the association. He was always the hands-on man, and I was more the behind-the-scenes helper who applied for state funds to improve the fairgrounds. A tornado destroyed the old fairgrounds on Highway 90, so the fair association decided to take the insurance money and buy property on Sand Path Road to construct a new fairground site.

The new fifty-seven-acre site, adjacent to Holmes County High School, took several years to develop. The county did most of the site work and did a good job getting the site ready for use. There was an old Department of Transportation barrow pit on the north side of the property that the fair board allowed the county to utilize as a dirt pit. The site had some of the most beautiful sand and clay of any pit around. The area was turned into a lake that added a great deal of value to the property. After years of service both Don and I retired from active duty with the fair association in 2011.

In the summer of 2013 the Holmes County School Board approached the board of commissioners about using the property to build a new school. As a result, the fair association has now disbanded and the county has agreed to deed the property to the school board for the new school.

I was a member of the Kiwanis club for over thirty years, and served as president in 1979. The Kiwanis rodeo is a big community event that has been a highlight for old and young alike since the late forties. It is held the first full weekend in October, and has a big two-day parade that thousands attend. The parade has had some very interesting entries throughout the years. The late Harvey Ethridge had a local radio program and was the parade chairman for many years. As he advertised the parade, he would announce to all who would listen that "if it's of interest to you, then your neighbors want to see it." George Howell, the owner of the local Chevrolet dealership and a character in his own right, said to Harvey one day, "There are some things that are of interest to me that I don't want my neighbors to see." Harvey just laughed and went right on with his parade announcement.

The club had a request from the owner of the Last Chance Bar, a local "juke joint," as my grandma would put it, to put a float in the parade advertising his business. The Kiwanis Board of Directors refused. Not to be outdone by the board, the guy just rented an eighteen wheeler and put a section of the bar on the flatbed trailer. Patrons were sitting right at the bar having a beer as the trailer was pulled through the parade route. Everyone got a big laugh, and the next year the club had to tighten up the parade rules.

In the late 1970s the government had a program called the Comprehensive Education and Training Act. The program was to help with unemployment in the country. The county was given several positions, and I asked the county commission to make one of them a county recreational director. Since it was my idea the position was placed under my supervision. The director and I discussed several programs for the county's youth and decided that reviving the little league was a good starting point. An organizational meeting was held, and there was a lot of interest in the program. Little league signup was a huge success, and the program had more teams than coaches. I was drafted to coach a team of eight- and nine-year-olds, and what an experience it was. It has been said that trying to coach kids this age is like trying to organize a can of earthworms, and that describes it pretty well.

I was a little league coach for many years. I started before my boys were old enough to play and continued until they grew out of little league age. My first team chose Red Sox as their name, and they were very successful. The team did not lose a game for the first two years.

Along with coaching, I was also the chief fund-raiser for the league. I called Mrs. Neal Blitch, a local restaurant owner, to ask her to sponsor a couple of uniforms for the Red Sox. She agreed to be the sponsor, and the team became Blitch's Red Sox. The team brought Mrs. Blitch championship trophies each year I coached. I still see some of my former players around town, and they remind me of the glory days of the Blitch's Red Sox.

* * *

CHAPTER 15

Bonifay Nursing Home

One day I was reading the newspaper, the Panama City *News Herald.* There was an article about a group applying for an addition to a nursing home in Marianna, Florida, in Jackson County, based on Holmes County's need. This was in the early 1980s, and the only nursing home that Holmes County had was an antiquated thirty-six-bed facility owned by Mrs. Lela Speed. It concerned me that another county was going to get Holmes County's beds and our citizens would have to go to Marianna, some thirty miles away, to a facility.

As a result of the article, I went by The First Bank of Holmes County, where Shouppe Howell was the president. I told him about the nursing home deal and suggested that he and I form a nonprofit group and apply for a certificate of need for additional beds for Holmes County. Mr. Howell looked across the desk and taught me the first of many financial lessons. He asked, "Why a nonprofit?" He said, "If it's worth doing, it needs to stay private." I told him that calling it "private" was fine with me. I called Mrs. Lela Speed, the owner of the old Bonifay Nursing Home; Kenneth Yates; and Gertrude Lee, the director of the county health department. They liked the idea and all agreed to be part of the new corporation, Holmes Health Care Inc. I was to be the president and Mr. Howell the vice president. The group authorized me to engage a local attorney to handle the incorporation. She prepared the paperwork, and I filed the papers in Tallahassee, Florida, and Holmes Health Care Inc. was officially in business.

The application for a certificate of need was huge, and it took several weeks to prepare. Mr. Howell, Mrs. Lee, and I did most of the application and finally sent it to the state agency to review. In a few months we got a form turndown letter from the department. I wrote a letter to Governor Bob Graham and informed him of what had happened, and a short time later I got a call from the governor's office telling us to resubmit our application. In another few months we got a letter of approval, giving us the right to build a sixty-bed nursing home.

We were like the dog that chased the car. When he caught it, he did not know what to do with it. The city of Bonifay agreed to help us do an Industrial Bond Issue. The bonds would not obligate the city. The city would be a conduit to help us get the financing, and the city in turn would get new jobs, a good customer, and an increase in its tax base. We found a contractor who could build the facility within the budget. He turned out to be a nice fellow but had his own ideas and timetables that did not coincide with ours as we worked to get things done. Finally after about a year we were able to complete the new Bonifay Nursing Home. I spent a great deal of time on the weekends and at night trying to keep the project going. The new home was opened in 1983. Shortly thereafter we were completely full. We decided to apply for another sixty beds, and we were successful, so we once again issued bonds to complete the second phase. Once the second phase was completed it too was quickly filled.

After Mrs. Speed died it became apparent that we would have to make some changes, and we decided to sell the home. I learned some valuable lessons from the experience, and now the new company has expanded the home to 180 beds. The nursing home is one of the largest employers in the county and provides care for those who need it. We were also able to keep people from our county from having to travel to another county for nursing home care. Of the original group, Kenneth Yates and I are the only survivors.

In addition to being a partner in the nursing home Gertrude and her husband Quincy were iconic Holmes County citizens. Not only did they live productively in the present, they preserved a bit of rural American that was quickly fading. When Gertrude Lee went to work at the Holmes County Health Department the county had one of the highest infant mortality rates in the state of Florida. She was the county health department director for many years and initiated programs to improve the health and survival rates of infants. Programs that she started improved the health of all county residents. She and her assistant, Ruby Bedford, went to all the schools in the county and administered routine vaccinations to everyone who needed them. Ms. Ruby was a wonderful, cheerful lady who happened to be black. She did more for race relations in our county than anyone I can think of.

By the time the schools were integrated in 1965, Ms. Ruby had been going to the schools for years with the health department. Everyone loved and respected her so much that integration seemed relatively easy. She would come to the class and announce the names of the students who needed vaccinations. As a youngster it was a strange feeling to see Ms. Ruby come to the door and call your name. Then she would take you back to the clinic, where Ms. Lee was waiting with a needle that looked like it was a foot long. Ms. Lee was a robust lady who would grab your arm and pop that needle in before you knew what was happening. In later years as I dealt with her as clerk, I would kid her that my heart still skipped a beat every time I saw her, thinking she might stab me one more time "for old times' sake."

Gertrude Lee was a former military nurse and when she spoke, the county commission listened. Not long after I was elected she came to see me about the county building a new health department. The health department had become the primary health care provider for many Holmes County citizens, and they were out of space. I told her to attend the next commission meeting and share her concerns with the board. She came to the next meeting, and before she left the board agreed to borrow the money to build a new health department from Farmers Home Administration. My staff filled out the forms, and the county was approved for the new facility. Because of her hard work and dedication to the citizens of the county I suggested to the county commission that it would be fitting to name the facility in her honor. In a surprise announcement, the building plaque was unveiled with the new health department's dedication. The department was named the Gertrude M. Lee Health Center. Ms. Lee was able to work her last few years before retiring in the building named in her honor.

Her husband, Quincy Lee, was present for the ceremony; Quincy was a colorful figure in his own right. Quincy Lee was a big man, and I do not mean fat. He was big boned, big on hard work and common sense, and big of heart. He was truly a "character," one of the last of a rare breed. He and Ms. Gertrude lived on the old family farm south of Bonifay that actually joined the Washington County line. He was just as much at home, or more so, in Washington County as Holmes. He was a deputy sheriff in Washington County until his retirement. He then became a full-time farmer, which was his real calling in life. If Quincy liked you, you knew it, and if he did not, you knew that too. He was just that kind of person. There was no pretense, no ulterior motives, and no effort to be anything or anybody but who he was, all day, every day.

I am not sure how I first got to know Quincy, but through the years I have dealt with him in several areas. I bought hay from him for my children's horses. The Lee farm was a throwback to the farms of yesteryear, complete with a cane mill and all types of farm animals. I took my children with me to get hay, just so they could see all the animals and the other things that Quincy had on the farm. On one trip to get hay I loaded twenty bales and stopped by to pay Quincy. I insisted that he go out and count the bales. He looked around and said, "I don't have to count; if I didn't trust you, I wouldn't be selling you hay." I laughed and paid him and went on my way.

Quincy also made the best sausage in the world. He, at one time, sold to the public, but the state wanted him to get licensed, be inspected, and fulfill the same heath requirements that big slaughterhouses had to, and he refused. The state investigator told him that if he sold any more sausage he would make a case against him. I often wondered where in Holmes or Washington County the state would find a jury that would convict the best sausage maker in the area. As time went by when Quincy made sausage he would call and never tell me who he was; he would just say, "You need to come and see me." I knew who it was. I would go down and pick up a supply for the next several months. The first time I went I wondered how we were going to make payment for the sausage since Quincy was under orders from the state not to sell sausage. I got the meat and asked Quincy, how much do I owe you?" He said, "You do not owe me anything." He then told me I could make a donation to help run the farm or give him a birthday present. Either of those would be fine, but remember, I did not owe him a thing for the sausage. I gave him a birthday present and went on my way

His passing a few years ago ended an era for this whole region. The farm from years gone by is not the same with the two of them gone. It will continue, however, in the hearts and minds of those of us fortunate enough to have known Gertrude and Quincy.

* * *

CHAPTER 16

OTHER THOUGHTS AND MUSINGS

I have indicated to a few close friends that I might write a book. Without exception all of them have encouraged me do so. Now that I have retired, the job of finishing the book has become reality. Brenda is my proofreader and advisor. Elizabeth Arnold proofed the court section for accuracy. Brenda and I have discussed what the title of the book should be. I first thought it should be *Order in the Court* but that leaves out all the other parts of the clerk's job. Brenda's sense of humor suggested, *Call in the Dogs and Put Out the Fire,* meaning it's all said and done, wrap it up, and go home. Whit vetoed that name. We next settled on *The Clerk,* and that seemed to cover it all.

As I get older I notice that people seem to listen to me more and actually take the advice I give. Prior to my retirement my employees treated me differently. They looked out for me, and they were quick to defend me and make sure that I looked good in every situation. I have a little bit of a hearing problem, and they covered for me to make sure I did not embarrass myself.

The hearing problem probably comes from not having ear protection when I worked at the Gold Kist Peanut Mill in Graceville, Florida, in the sixties. We would operate the big suction pipe to unload the peanuts, and at the end of a shift our ears would ring for hours. Firing weapons in basic training and dove hunting without ear protection did not help either. Luke and I were going on a trip one day, and he asked me a question. I answered a completely different question from the one he had asked me. He had to speak up and ask me again. He looked over at me and said, "You need a Beltone." My answer to him was, "I have a belt on." He just laughed and kept going.

I also am beginning to do things that I saw my grandparents do. As a boy I never could understand why anyone would want to sit on the front porch in a swing or sit by a fire in the winter. Guess what, I now love to sit on the front porch in my swing with a ceiling fan overhead and just enjoy listening to the radio or watching the cats, birds, and grandchildren play. Brenda wants a fire on every cold day in the winter, and it is a full-time job keeping firewood on the fire. I have tried to get her to let me get a gas or electric insert, but she will not have it.

Tree watching, as you might call it, has become another pleasurable activity for me. I notice the different trees in the spring as they come to life starting in early February. Red maple trees are the first ones that bloom in their many shades of red. Their tiny leaves trick you into thinking they are blooms as they appear on those bare limbs. But almost as you watch, those tiny red dots cast against the still gray of winter become miniature green leaves that mature into the lovely maple leaf. I also love the trees as they begin to turn in the fall, and I marvel at how beautiful they are. The red, orange, and yellow show is just breathtaking. I guess I just enjoy the beauty of God's creation each day.

Health issues are of greater concern now than when I was younger and didn't give a lot of thought to them. I tend to notice the ailments and pains that my friends have, and I have a few of my own. As I see people my age having health problems and in some cases dying, it really makes me aware of my own mortality. I am learning to appreciate every day that I have been blessed with and try to enjoy it to the fullest. I try to have my priorities in order by having my life right with God, and since he ordained the family ahead of everything but Him, I try to spend more time with my family. I go to some public functions but not as many as I did at one time. If it conflicts with a family matter, the family comes first. Having grandchildren changes one's total outlook on life.

I find that I get more emotional with age, and even though I previously thought that a man was never supposed to cry, I sometimes find myself doing so in special situations. When I gave Hilary away at her wedding I made it fine until just before we went in, and then it almost overwhelmed me. I could hardly speak when they ask who was giving this woman in marriage. When Brenda and I went with Hilary to get the results of her dental school state boards, she opened the envelope, and when we saw that she passed, we just stood there and cried because we were so happy and relieved.

Working outside brings a unique sort of joy. I enjoy cutting my grass and bush hogging the pasture in front of our home. Bush hogging is relaxing. Several years ago Brenda asked me to let her try bush hogging, and I showed her how. Since then she has taken over. She says she now realizes why I loved it so. She actually does a better job than I did. She has replaced Luke and me as the operator of the bush hog. She says it is like boating on land, and since she has never had a boat, it is a great substitute. She also says it is a wonderful thing to actually see the immediate results of your labor. You can look back over your shoulder and see those neatly cut swaths that eventually give you a totally smooth, rolling pasture. It's unlike her previous job of school counselor, where you could never be certain of the outcome of your labor. I told her the other day I was going to introduce her to the grease gun and the diesel fuel can. She informed me that she only does the driving, not the maintenance on the equipment. So I do the maintenance and she does the driving.

Thankfully Hilary graduated from dental school in May of 2008 and I have been successful in getting back the last of the gas credit cards from my children. Now that is quite an accomplishment. I told Brenda that life is unfair—you should make the most money when you are young. That is when you need to build a home and would like to travel. Now that we are older, the children are grown and out on their own, and financially we have the means to go a few places, we are not that anxious to go. Just getting to see our children and grandchildren, going to church, taking a little day trip or shopping for the day, and eating out occasionally make us happy. We have decided that happiness is found in the small things of life and is expressed in how you live life each day.

It is amazing to me that as I get older some of the things that I thought were bedrock ideas have begun to change. For instance I no longer think that you should put people in jail and throw away the key. I now think that we have gone too far in Florida with prison sentencing. Florida went over one hundred thousand in prison population last year. I now am of the opinion that most jail sentences are too long. Florida incarcerated almost as many inmates last year as did the whole federal system. As a result, The

Florida Department of Corrections is requiring more and more of the state budget.

Legislators find themselves in the position of making hard decisions, such as cutting funds for education, nursing homes, and Medicaid in deference to providing more money for prisons. Most elected officials do not want to be viewed as soft on crime, and that is why it is hard to get the legislature to do away with sentencing guidelines and other mandatory sentences that fill up correctional institutions and require that new ones be built. I told former senator Durelle Peaden that he should support doing away with the mandatory sentences, and he looked at me like I was crazy. I told him he would not be soft on crime because he would not be letting off anyone who was already on death row. All the sex offenders would have a standing reservation, and the violent criminals would also have a prison bed, but anyone other than those included in these three groups should be left to the discretion of judges. If judges are too lenient, voters can replace them through the election process. The legislature has no choice but to look at ways to decrease the prison population as they are faced with shrinking revenues.

I have always loved history; that is why I majored in political science and went back and got my master's degree in public administration. I love to read Washington, Jefferson, and others. Washington's farewell address has almost convinced me to become nonpartisan. His warning about what happens when one puts party ahead of country is so prophetic.

I wrote a letter to the chairperson of the Florida Democratic Party and told her that I would never sign another loyalty oath to a political party. I told her that I would sign an oath to my family, my God, and my country, but never again to a political party. She never answered me, so I do not know if I am out of the party or not. It has always been strange to me that both major parties require their members to sign a loyalty oath swearing that they will support the party nominee regardless of who it is. That is the most undemocratic thing I have ever heard of. I vote for the person I believe to be the best qualified regardless of which party he or she is a member of. (See appendix C.) I hope to see the day that officeholders will do what is best for America and not the party. Much of the gridlock in Washington is because of the allegiance to a political party.

Of all the founding fathers, I love Jefferson's writings best. His predictions about taxation and spending have come true. I look around and see all the financial problems our nation is having caused by nothing but unmitigated greed. The financial burden we are placing on our children and grandchildren really bothers me. It is strange that you never hear anyone in Washington talk about an austerity package. The Congress does know, however, how to borrow, borrow, and borrow. I wonder sometimes how much the Chinese and other countries will loan us before they literally own us.

Some people in Washington talk about how great Jefferson was. His suggestions on dealing with a government out of control are eye opening. I hesitate to put what he said into words for fear that some may take them as mine. So with the disclaimer that these words belong to Jefferson and not me, here I go. He said, "The tree of liberty must be refreshed from time to time with the blood of patriots and tyrants." [iii] Whether he meant to get rid of the rascals by the ballot box or other means is left to the interpretation of the readers of Jefferson.

I do not worry for myself when I see the conditions that exist in America today. I do worry for my children and my grandchildren.

All the things that my generation grew up believing were right have seemingly gone by the wayside. It seems that the belief of today is that God had nothing to do with the formation of America and has no place in its future. The family unit as we knew is hard to recognize.

We live in a world turned upside down. The only thing that can right this is for America to turn back to God. It is only through his guidance, love, patience, and mercy that we have any hope for the salvation and renewal of our country.

* * *

CHAPTER 17

The Next Chapter

Decision Time

In the fall of 2011 I spent some time trying to decide whether or not to run again. This term marked thirty-six years as clerk. Prior to being elected clerk I had almost six months active duty with the Florida National Guard, almost three years as assistant county agent, and two years as a right-of-way agent with The Florida Department of Transportation. I was sixty-four in February of 2013, and that made me realize that I needed to retire and travel and do some things that I have always wanted to do.

Brenda thinks that I will be bored by retirement and thinks I will not like the freedom of suddenly having nothing to do. I remind her that helping raise grandchildren will keep us busy. After much prayer and careful consideration I decided on February 6, 2012, that I would retire. I made the announcement to my staff on February 7, 2012, and gave them the speech that I had practiced so many times but was not exactly ready to deliver. I have peace about the decision; I have been blessed with good health and look forward to another phase of my life. I have had several folks tell me to run again and come in part time. That is not me. Being the clerk of court in a small county is a full-time job and needs someone's best effort.

I made the public announcement of my retirement, and with Elizabeth Arnold's help I made a final report to the citizens of the county. The report, included in the appendix, is a summary of the major activities during my thirty-six years in office. (See appendix D, D2.)

All the grandchildren came to visit on July 4, 2012, and what a time it was. If the visit is any indication of the retirement years, things should be lively. The worse part of the visits is the parting. It is always heart-wrenching to hug those little ones good-bye until the next time.

Since I have announced my retirement many people have been so kind. Folks have gone out of their way to tell me how sad they are that I am retiring but glad for me because I can travel and enjoy the grandchildren. One of our more outspoken citizens came by to see me the other day and said he just wanted to shake the hand of the man who had enough backbone to get out of the public trough all by himself without the voters having to put him out. We had a big laugh, and he went on his way. Another friend came by on my last day in office to offer me some advice. He told me to travel and spend as much of Brenda's and my savings as we could. He ended his advice by telling me to let the funeral director inform the children about the reverse mortgage when he handed them the funeral bill. We do plan to travel but will probably forgo the remainder of his recommendation.

Congressman Jeff Miller presented me with a certificate of service that he had read into the Congressional Record. (See appendix E, E2, E3.) One of his aides presented me the certificate at my last county commissioner meeting. I include it mostly for my grandchildren to see how great Papa really is.

Many people asked me during the election who I recommended as my replacement. My standard answer was that the voters of Holmes County had used extremely good judgment in electing their clerk for the past thirty-six years. I figured that they would continue to do so in the future. I would not insult their intelligence by telling them how to vote.

My deputy clerks held a retirement dinner for me at Old Mill Restaurant in Dothan, Alabama, on November 3, 2012. They invited as a surprise guest my friend and fellow clerk, Rickey Lyons, and his wife, Louisa. Two of my children and four of my grandchildren were also present. It was a very nice occasion, one that will leave enduring memories for Brenda and me.

On November 6, 2012, the voters of Holmes County elected my replacement, Kyle Hudson. He had previously been employed as an agriculture teacher at Ponce de Leon High School and seems to be well suited to be clerk. We experienced a smooth transition. On January 7, 2013, the auditors were present at closing. They checked me out, and I turned over the keys to the office. I told my staff good-bye and walked out the door for the last time as clerk. That night at twelve o'clock, my term as clerk was over and my retirement began.

Helping Brenda run the daycare for five of our grandchildren has been a challenge. Taylor, Eli, Brighton, Georgia, and Abram are all under five years of age. They keep things interesting to say the least. Brenda says I am rough around the edges, but that I am making progress as her newest and only daycare assistant.

Sunset

As I approached the sunset of my political career, I often reflected on the responsibility that the citizens of Holmes County gave a young man, twenty-seven years old, and a dedicated group of employees. The memories of past campaigns and the things that I dealt with in the clerk's office are forever branded in my mind. I want the citizens of the county to say that I guarded the checkbook like it was my own, I did what I could to help every person who sought help, and that the office was in better shape when I left than when I arrived. It's indeed time to "call in the dogs and put out the fire."

* * *

Epilogue

I received a call in December of 2013 informing me that Linda Cook, the clerk of court in neighboring Washington County, had retired because of health problems. The caller wanted to know if I would be interested in the job. I told him I needed to talk it over with Brenda and would get back to him. The novelty of being the clerk in two different counties did intrigue me a little, but we quickly decided that I did not want to get back into the day-to-day stress of the clerk's office. I called the person back and told him that I would decline. I enjoy the schedule that Brenda and I have and just could not give up ten or eleven months to get back in the everyday grind. I told Taylor about the offer one day as I picked him up at school. He said, "Papa, I don't want you to do what that man wants you to do. You need to be at home, with your young'uns." I thought that was pretty good advice from a four-year-old.

APPENDIX A

WILLIAM N. MEGGS
STATE ATTORNEY

LEON COUNTY COURTHOUSE
301 S. MONROE STREET
TALLAHASSEE, FLORIDA 32399-2550

TELEPHONE (850) 488-6701

OFFICE OF
STATE ATTORNEY
SECOND JUDICIAL CIRCUIT OF FLORIDA

December 17, 2002

Governor Jeb Bush
Office of the Governor
Room 209, The Capitol
Tallahassee, FL 32399-0001

ATTN: Tena Pate

RE: Executive Order #02-298 (Extension of Executive Orders #00-347 & 01-340)
Holmes County

Dear Governor Bush:

This office has completed our responsibility under the above Executive Assignment. Investigator Wayne Hicks conducted a thorough investigation and found no evidence of fraud. (See enclosed newspaper article.) This office kept our investigation open pending the results of a civil suit filed by a candidate in Holmes County. A Final Judgment has been entered dismissing the civil suit (see enclosed). The Final Judgment entered on December 9, 2002 is self explanatory.

Thank you for the confidence that you placed in this office. I regret the length of our assignment, but we elected to wait for the results of the civil case in the event we may have missed something.

Sincerely,

William N Meggs

WILLIAM N. MEGGS
State Attorney

WNM/jw
Enclosures

cc: Honorable Jim Appleman
State Attorney
Fourteenth Judicial Circuit

RECEIVED

DEC 19 2002

WILLIAM N. MEGGS
STATE ATTORNEY

TALLAHASSEE
Suite 200
1500 Mahan Drive
Tallahassee, Florida 32308
(850) 224-4070 Tel
(850) 224-4073 Fax

Nabors Giblin & Nickerson P.A.
ATTORNEYS AT LAW

FORT LAUDERDALE
1225 S.E. Second Avenue
Fort Lauderdale, Florida 33316
(954) 525-8000 Tel
(954) 525-8331 Fax

TAMPA
Suite 1060
2502 Rocky Point Drive
Tampa, Florida 33607
(813) 281-2222 Tel
(813) 281-0129 Fax

April 7, 2008

Cody Taylor
Clerk of Courts
Holmes County
3268 Cody Taylor Lane
Bonifay, Florida 32425

Dear Cody:

As we discussed, enclosed is a copy of your letter, dated May 26, 1981, to Governor Bob Graham raising issues relating to restraints on county funding.

I served as General Counsel to Governor Graham for a six-month period in the first half of 1981 and as Special Counsel for Legislative Affairs during 1982 when Governor Graham decided to seek a one cent increase in the state sales tax.

During this time, I also was in private practice and served as contract attorney to the Board of County Commissioners of Brevard County, Florida.

I have kept this letter all these years because of its special place in county funding efforts during this period. Your letter was read, taken seriously by Governor Graham and had a profound influence on his understanding of the funding plights faced by small Florida counties. To a large degree, your letter was the trigger that prompted Governor Graham to seek a one half local option sales tax for counties in 1981. Such efforts were unsuccessful but Governor Graham pressed on during the 1982 Legislative Session (an election year) to seek a one cent increase in the sales tax to be partially applied to ad valorem property tax relief and to provide fiscal support to Florida local governments. Such efforts, after numerous special sessions, resulted in the adoption of the half cent local government sales tax codified in Chapter 218, Florida Statutes. An integral part of the passage of such 1982 sales tax increase was the incorporation of what was referred to then as the "small county kicker" which evolved into the various small county surtaxes.

As I mentioned earlier, the enclosed letter of May 26, 1981, had a profound influence on Governor Graham to undertake the aggressive and politically risky pursuit of these tax reforms that ultimately provided direct fiscal assistance to small counties.

Cody Taylor
April 7, 2008
Page 2

You and your family should be proud of your efforts at this crucial period in Florida's history. Your letter is a testament to the fact that dedicated people can make a difference by speaking up.

I look forward to seeing you again in the near future.

Very truly yours,

Bob

Robert L. Nabors

RLN/adm

Enclosure

F:\Tally Data\General Data\WPDATA\rln\Taylor4_2.doc

Office Of

CLERK OF CIRCUIT COURT
HOLMES COUNTY

201 N. Oklahoma St. Bonifay, Florida 32425

CODY TAYLOR
Clerk

May 26, 1981

Honorable Bob Graham, Governor
State of Florida
The Capitol
Tallahassee, Florida 32301

Dear Governor Graham:

I watched your news conference last week and would like to let you know my reaction to it. I am the Clerk to the Board of County Commissioners in Holmes County and as I listened to you name the areas that the legislature had not funded I did not hear you mention counties. I agree that we need to fund education, law enforcement, community care for the elderly and transportation. The one area you seem to have overlooked is the plight of counties and cities.

Holmes County, last year lost over $35,000 with the increased homestead exemption passed by the people of Florida. This occured after the Board went to 10 mills. The roll-back rate for the County was 10.3 mills. This year, after the additional homestead exemption is taken from our tax roll we anticipate $3,000,000 net growth. After the loss of the local government exemption trust fund we will have another decrease in revenue this year.

We would have no objection to cutting back in some areas, but what makes it so hard for counties to operate is budget items that we have no control over. The increase in the County's share of the Medicaid program goes up each year. It has gotten to the point we cannot afford to pay it. We have already been threatened by the collection department. They have notified the Comptroller to withhold our State Revenue Sharing Fund. They will just have to withhold them, because with the spending caps imposed the last two years and now the revenue losses we cannot pay what they bill us. The Medicaid program should be funded by Congress and the legislature not by counties.

I do not believe that you or the legislature realize the problems the counties are encountering. We must have help just to maintain the status quo. When we levy all the property taxes we can levy we have nowhere else to go, but to the legislature.

Honorable Bob Graham
Page 2
May 26, 1981

The legislature has never assumed its' share of the costs of Article V. The counties are left to pick up the tab for part of Medical Examiners fees, witness fees, filing fees for the indigent and Attorney fees for the indigent. I think you can see all of these are State functions and should be funded by the State.

What we really ask is to be treated in the same light as the priorities you mentioned in your news conference. When the exemption on School property went to $25,000 the legislature created a trust fund to reimburse schools for a portion or all of the money they lost. The services we provide are just as important to our citizens and we must have help to replace lost revenue.

Sir, I hope you see that we in County and City government have our backs to the wall. We must have your help and the help of the legislature to be able to provide the services our citizens deserve. You may have addressed some of these problems in your budget and I hope you have. Hopefully we can count on you to help us through these difficult times.

Sincerely yours,

Cody Taylor

Cody Taylor
Clerk

CT:skb

cc: Honorable Dempsey Barron
Honorable Pat Thomas
Honorable Sam Mitchell

APPENDIX C

August 25, 2005

Karen L. Thurman, Chair
Florida Democratic Party
Post Office Box 1758
Tallahassee, Florida 32302

Ms. Thurman:

I received your letter of August 16 informing me that I was an automatic delegate to the Florida Democratic Convention to be held in Orlando in December. Please be advised that I hereby revoke any and all loyalty oaths to the Florida Democratic Party if any, and will never sign another loyalty oath to any political party. You say you want to change the Florida Democratic Party to make it more inclusive. Why don't you do away with a loyalty oath? This oath is one of the most un-democratic things I have ever heard of.

The new policy should be that we ask people to vote their conscience. If we cannot put forth candidates that people would want to vote for as a matter of conscience, we do not deserve to expect voters to vote for our candidates.

I will be glad to sign a loyalty oath to my God, my family or my country, but from this day forth I will vote the vote of conscience. I will vote for the person that I feel in my heart is best for America. I wish you would read George Washington's farewell address and what he warned about political parties and you would see that what he predicted is true. When people put party ahead of country you have nothing but political bickering.

Please convey this revocation of the loyalty oath to anyone who may need it.

Sincerely Yours,

Cody Taylor

Cody Taylor
Clerk

Office of
Clerk of Circuit Court
Holmes County

Cody Taylor
Clerk

P.O. Box 397
Bonifay, FL 32425

Dear Citizens of Holmes County:

It has been a pleasure to serve as your Clerk of the Circuit Court, County Court, County Recorder and County Auditor since January, 1977.

I have served with very dedicated and loyal Deputy Clerks; without whose service the Clerk's Office would not have been nearly as efficient.

Please allow me the opportunity to provide you the following summary of the services provided by the Clerk's Office from January 1977 thru December 31, 2012.

Circuit Court

Deputy Clerks in the Circuit Court Division of the Clerk's Office have filed and processed 32,092 cases. These include Felony and Juvenile Delinquency cases in the Criminal Division, as well as Civil, Domestic Relations, Probate, Guardianship and Juvenile Dependency cases in the Civil Division.
These Deputy Clerks have also processed hundreds of Child Support payments and Judgments for delinquent child support payments, summonsed and processed payment for thousands of Jurors and Witnesses as requested by the Courts, attended hundreds of court proceedings and prepared minutes for all proceedings.
Pleadings filed in Circuit Court cases are now imaged and dockets for all Circuit Court cases are available on the Clerk's Website.
E-filing through the Myflorida.com e-portal has been implemented for all Circuit Civil cases, including Probate.

County Court

Deputy Clerks in the County Court Division of the Clerk's Office have filed and processed 39,450 cases. These include Misdemeanor and Criminal Traffic cases in the Criminal Division, as well as Civil and Traffic Infractions in the Civil Division.
These Deputy Clerks have also issued witness subpoenas for hundreds of traffic hearings as well as processed thousands of D-6s for failure to pay traffic fines.
Pleadings filed in County Court cases are now imaged and dockets for all County Court cases are available on the Clerk's Website.
E-filing through the Myflorida.com e-portal has been implemented for all County Civil cases.

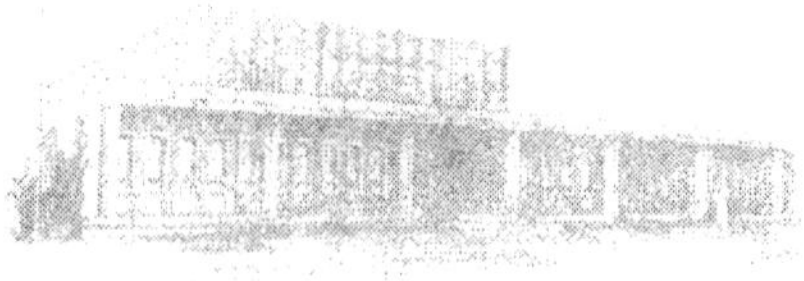

County Recorder

Deputy Clerks in the Recording Division have recorded and indexed over 431,000 pages of Deeds, Mortgages, and other property-related documents into the Official Records of Holmes County. Documents are now accepted for e-filing through the Myflorida.com e-portal. These Deputy Clerks have also microfilmed these records for off-site storage, or imaged over 30 years of these Official Records which are available on the Clerk's Website. Paper copies of all Official Records are available in the Clerk's Office.
Several Subdivision Plats have been filed and indexed by these Deputy Clerks and are stored in the Clerk's Office.
Approximately 4,700 Marriage Licenses have been issued and processed by these Deputy Clerks, as well as hundreds of Marriage Ceremonies performed.
Thousands of Passport Applications have been accepted, processed and submitted to the Passport Agency by this Department.
Over Three Hundred Tax Deed Applications were accepted, processed, sales held, and proceeds disbursed by Deputy Clerks.

County Auditor

Under my supervision as County Auditor and Budget Officer, Deputy Clerks have been responsible for preparing and administering budgets for the Board of County Commissioners and the Clerk of Court. These Deputy Clerks have worked with budgets for the Board of County Commissioners that range from $1,560,382.74 for budget year 1976-77 to $23,124,610.00 for the 2007-08 budget year, with the current 2012-13 budget being $17,029,151.00. All bills have been paid on time and all budgets have been balanced during my 36 year tenure as Clerk.
Hundreds of Board of County Commissioner meetings have been attended by Myself or a Deputy Clerk and minutes of all meetings were prepared. Minutes of County Commission Meetings since 2006 are currently available on the Clerk's website.

I hope that you find this summary informative.

It has been an honor to serve as your Clerk of Courts and Auditor for the past 36 years.

My staff and I are preparing for a smooth transition to the new Clerk that you have chosen.

May God bless you and your Family.

In your service I remain,

Cody Taylor

Cody Taylor
Clerk of Court
January 3, 1977 – January 7, 2013

Congressional Record

PROCEEDINGS AND DEBATES OF THE *112th* CONGRESS, SECOND SESSION

The Honorable Jeff Miller of the First District of Florida
Washington, Friday, September 21, 2012

RECOGNIZING THE SERVICE OF NORTHWEST FLORIDA'S CODY TAYLOR

Speaker, I rise today to recognize Cody Taylor, on the occasion of his retirement after thirty-six years of service as Clerk of Court for Holmes County, Florida. For more than three decades, Mr. Taylor served the citizens of Northwest Florida with distinction and unwavering commitment to public service.

A native of Northwest Florida, Mr. Taylor attended Poplar Spring High School in Graceville. There, he helped lead the basketball team to two state championships. He received a basketball scholarship to Chipola Junior College and to the University of West Florida, where he graduated with a bachelor's degree in Political Science and a master's degree in Public Administration. In 1976, Mr. Taylor was elected Holmes County Clerk. He has served in this capacity with the utmost respect and integrity. His tireless work ethic and dedication to the citizens of Holmes County for the last thirty-six years did not go unnoticed. In 2007, Mr. Taylor was named the "Clerk of the Year" by the Florida Association of Court Clerks and Comptrollers.

Mr. Taylor's commitment to the Northwest Florida community extends well beyond his role as Holmes County Clerk of Court. He is an active member of the Holmes County Chamber of Commerce and a

devoted member of the First Baptist Church. Mr. Taylor served in the Florida Army National Guard and as a member of the Bonifay Kiwanis Club and West Florida Regional Planning Council. For twenty years, he served as a member of the Bonifay Little League Association and as a basketball official for the Florida High School Athletic Association. He was also the President and Board Member of the Holmes County Fair Association, President and co-founder of Holmes Healthcare, and Vice President of the Florida Future Farmers of America.

In addition to his service to the community, Mr. Taylor is also a loving and committed husband, father and grandfather. He and his wife Brenda, also a Northwest Florida native, have four children, Zachary, Whit, Lucas, and Hilary; and eleven grandchildren, Jordan, Jacob, Jackson, Kodie, Campbell, Graham, Gwynneth, Eli, Taylor, Brighton, and Georgia. I know Mr. Taylor looks forward to spending more time with them following his retirement.

Mr. Speaker, on behalf of the United States Congress, I thank Cody Taylor for his dedication to our community, and I congratulate him on his retirement. My wife, Vicki and I wish him and his family all the best.

[i] Carswell, E. W. *Holmesteading, The History of Holmes County, Florida.* Tallhassee: Rose Printing Company, 1986. Pages 7–9.

[ii] "Give 'em Hell, Harry! Quotes." Net. Stands 4 LLC, 2014. Web 24 April, 2014. <http://www.quotes.net/movies/Give'em Hell Harry:>

[iii] Larson, Nathan. Jefferson, Magnificent Populist. Washington: Robert B. Luce, Inc. 1981. Pages 35–36.

61500161R00122

Made in the USA
Lexington, KY
12 March 2017